Ruling Illusions:
Philosophy and the Social Order

PHILOSOPHY NOW:

General Editor: Roy Edgley

English-speaking philosophy since the Second World War has been dominated by the method of linguistic analysis, the latest phase of the analytical movement started in the early years of the century. That method is defined by certain doctrines about the nature and scope both of philosophy and of the other subjects from which it distinguishes itself; and those doctrines reflect the fact that in this period philosophy and other intellectual activities have been increasingly monopolised by the universities, social institutions with a special role. Though expansive in the number of practitioners, these activities have cultivated an expertise that in characteristic ways has narrowed their field of vision. As our twentieth-century world has staggered from crisis to crisis, English-speaking philosophy in particular has submissively dwindled into a humble academic specialism, on its own understanding isolated from the practical problems facing society, and from contemporary Continental thought.

The books in this series are united by nothing except discontent with this state of affairs. Convinced that the analytical movement has spent its momentum, its latest phase no doubt its last, the series seeks in one way or another to push philosophy out of its ivory tower.

Other books in the series:

Philosophy and its Past
Jonathan Rée, Michael Ayers, Adam Westoby

Art an Enemy of the People
Roger Taylor

Sartre
Istvan Meszaros

The Possibility of Naturalism
Roy Bhaskar

Note: this series was originally published by Sussex University Press, and two titles are available from them: Benjamin Gibbs, *Freedom and Liberation;* Richard Norman, *Hegel's Phenomenology*.

Ruling Illusions:
Philosophy and the Social Order

ANTHONY SKILLEN
Keynes College, University of Kent

THE HARVESTER PRESS

First published in 1977 by
THE HARVESTER PRESS LIMITED
Publisher: John Spiers
2 Stanford Terrace, Hassocks, Sussex

British Library Cataloguing in Publication Data

Skillen, Anthony
    Ruling illusions - (Philosophy now).
    1. Political science
    I. Title II. Series
    320'.01   B65

    ISBN 0-85527-880-3 (cloth)
    ISBN 0-85527-890-0 (paper)

Photoset by LPS Graphics Ltd., Purley
and printed in England by
Redwood Burn Ltd., Trowbridge and Esher

Contents

Introduction
THE KINGDOM OF ENDS AND THE END OF KINGDOMS

Chapter One
PHILOSOPHICAL STATISM

The Logic of Loyalty   12
The Statist Conception of Politics   22
Politics as Superstructure: Marx   27
Levels of Politics   40

Chapter Two
THE POLITICS OF PRODUCTION

Labour: Philosophy's Suppressed Premiss   45
Free Slavery: Wage-Labour in Capitalist Society   55
Labour as Fulfilment: Job-Enrichment   68
Towards Democratic Industry   85

Chapter Three
FORENSIC PHILOSOPHY

The Discreet Violence of Bourgeois Law   91
Legitimation Through Sublimation: Hart's *Concept of Law* 93
The Law as White Man's Magic   102
Natural Law: or the Prudent Despot   107
'Philosophy of Punishment': the Soft Sell of the Hard Cell 109

Chapter Four
MORALISM AND MORALITY

Moral Philosophy in the Academy   122
The Bureaucrat and the Beast: The Dualities of Moralism 129
Radical Anti-Moralism from Hegel to Reich   147
Cheap Government: The Political Economy of Bourgeois Virtue 151

Acknowledgements

This book has developed from talks and articles (in *Radical Philosophy*) since 1970 and has benefited from many criticisms and suggestions particularly from Larry Blum, G.A. and J.M. Cohen, Andrew Collier, Gerald Doppelt, Roy Edgley, George Molnar, Richard Norman and Sean Sayers.

INTRODUCTION

THE KINGDOM OF ENDS AND THE END OF KINGDOMS

Mornings at English infants schools begin with Assembly. Hymns and prayers are rendered and offered. Parents, most of them uninvolved in explicit piety, are either indifferent or approving. The songs are 'nice', 'it brings them together', 'it's a way of making them behave'. True. But there is more to it than that: a general mode of education and the particular twist given it by a particular headmistress are ritually consecrated, daily represented, as embodiments of the absolute authority of the All Wise God. So it is that the rules enjoining boys to wear (short) trousers and Girls to wear (not too short) dresses are lent the dignity of Natural Law. So it is, moreover, that assembling is experienced as an essentially official phenomenon - and one might almost say, after Jubilee Year, that the English have come to experience festivity as an essentially *royal* phenomenon, blessing the Queen for street parties that year instead of wondering why they do not 'happen' rather more frequently. Monarchy lends rarity a crown! In other words, what is contingent is presented as necessary, what is accidental is presented as essential. Philosophy, bad philosophy, is at large. It lives in the institutions of our lives. The purpose of this book, (which will contain no doubt its own measure of bad philosophy) is to highlight this fact and to bring home some of the ways in which the established, implicit, philosophies of our schools, states, companies, law-courts, prisons and families are reproduced and supported by what is explicitly accredited as 'Philosophy' in our universities.

Statism, Managerialism, Legalism and Moralism are 'philosophies', or aspects of philosophies, in which dominant forces are abstracted out, idealised, clothed in laundered white samite - 'mystic, wonderful' - and offered to us as the things that can save us from that from which they were abstracted - disorder, anarchy, lawlessless and violence. I shall try to bring out a pervasive distortion in these philosophies, a distortion marked in general terms by 'dualism', by the erection of a higher order-of-being whose function it is to correct base nature. But if there are solutions to life's problems, life has to provide them.

Immanuel Kant wrote of a Kingdom of Ends to which the true 'Self', transcendental exerciser of the Moral Will, belonged. But, in rescuing for a higher domain the bearer of true dignity and worth, Kant simultaneously consigned the lowly empirical self, passionately and bodily trapped in the world of earthly affairs, to even more certain indignity and worthlessness. So it had been with Plato's forms, perfect paradigms of perfection, which were supposed to explain their earthly approximations as well as to guide them toward ever closer resemblances of themselves. Having divided the world thus into pure and impure reality, Plato, as he seems to have recognised in *The Parmenides,* could not reunite it: either there had to be muddy imperfections among the forms themselves to explain the muddy imperfections in material things, or earthly things had to be credited with form and value in their own right, making the forms redundant.

Kant and Plato, now as always, have always been criticised for their dualism. But their 'kingdoms', their 'ultimates', their entities which moved things without being moved by things, which dealt with evil without being penetrated by evil, and which functioned to bring order to that which was by nature unordered, live on. Despite the official demise of 'Idealism' and of 'Rationalism', the hierarchical, even monarchistic mode of thinking continues to pervade especially the royal family of 'Political', 'Legal' and 'Moral' philosophy. As the British monarch is presented to us as the central embodiment and focus of all that the British hold dear in these and all other troubled times - as the incarnate form of Britishness - State, Law and Morality are displayed in the loyal philosophical text of the academic philosophers as special sources of good order in human life. These monarchial fallacies' it is this book's aim to expose.

The royal style draws its sustenance from a hierarchical, Christian, capitalist culture. Industry, production, play a negligible part in the standard philosophy texts; yet, as I shall argue, it is the hierarchial structure of working life, and particularly the fact of orchestrated drudgery, that provides the cornerstone of an understanding of the dualistic forms in which philosophers celebrate the state and pontificate about morality. It was not for nothing that Plato's construction of the 'just' state and the 'just' soul in *The Republic* begins with a defence of specialist hierarchy in the organisation of production.

Dualisms reinforce one another. Itself a product of the wider departmentalism of bourgeois culture, the serene and majestic isolation of modern academic philosophy departments helps maintain the monarchical tradition, the idea of 'special bodies' wondrously suited to run things. Despite attacks from within, it is still orthodox to present philosophy as concerned, not with 'facts', but with 'concepts'; not with 'the world', but with 'how we talk about the world'; not with whether or not something is the case, - for example whether abortion is infanticide, - but with 'what it means to say that it is, or is not'. Among the many objectionable things about this apartheid is this: unless philosophy is concerned to understand reality and to seek the categories, forms or concepts in terms of which things and processes can be realistically understood; unless philosophy refuses to confine itself to 'talk about talk' whose relation to what it is talk *about* is not considered, its tendency must be to tidy up, to 'rationalise' the dominant discourses and to leave untouched their claims to articulate the way the world is.

Language — words and other symbolic expressions such as architecture - actively structures perceptions of reality and hence actively structures social reality itself. The very terms of political argument, for example, are a part of politics, and the very emergence of a form of words as the 'accepted' characterisation of a political state of affairs (is it a 'clique'?, a 'régime'?, a 'government'?) distils and further shapes political activity and struggle. That is why philosophy, as the activity of 'critique' of discourse, cannot confine itself to the level of discourse, still less to official discourse, and cannot limit itself to delineating 'meanings', pointing out ambiguities and so on. Rather must it strive to grasp the relationship

of discourse and reality, to examine the adequacy of categori-
sations, ways of conceiving, 'philosophies', that are em-
bodied in human talking, thinking and acting. That means,
not that philosophy must disappear - the philosophical
ignorance of the sciences is but the reverse-side of the
empirical ignorance of the philosophers - but that it must
abandon its courtly isolation, its celebration of 'second-
order' status and its self-congratulatory ignorance of the world
Philosophy is an indispensable dimension of scientific activity.

In his *Philosophical Investigations*, Wittgenstein urged
philosophers to get off their one-sided diet of official philosophical terms and examples and to explore the living complex-
ity of language as embedded in whole 'forms of life'. He
thought that such exploration would, properly focused,
'dissolve' the problems with which the philosophers were
torturing themselves; that 'the facts' of living discourse
would mock the grandiose urges of philosophers. But he did
not propose that this living discourse is itself susceptible to
criticism by 'the facts', for he seems to have thought of
discourse as constituting its facts. Thus, for all his calls to
earth, Wittgenstein, more resolutely than the 'empiricists, he
attacked, sought to protect discourse from philosophical
criticism, and to blind us to tensions, both within 'forms of
life' and between those 'forms' and what they may impose
on. It is all very well, for example, to say of 'moral discourse'
that 'this game is played', but this does not face the problem
that the playing of this game involves arguable and contested
presuppositions about the springs of human action, about the
will, and about what holds people together. Nor does it face
the problem that it can be a central part of a 'form of life' to
claim a unique validity and hence the right to supplant others
-think of Christianity -so that the conceptual permissiveness
of saying that each 'language game' can be examined within
its own terms leads to a self-contradictory acceptance-and-
rejection of such imperialist games. Wittgenstein tried to
bring philosophy down to earth, but in declaring the earth
constituted by language, he left it, and philosophy, up in the
air. No wonder, despite the social conception of concepts
that he advanced, that Wittgenstein steered clear of conceptual politics.

In this book I try to bring out the extent to which professional academic philosophers, as well as philosophising 'social scientists', make thinking about things—trying to sort out the right way to understand things; philosophy - difficult. I try to bring out a pervasive 'idealism', an idealisation of certain institutions - as if they could be grasped, *a priori,* as embodying the attributes proclaimed in their labels, - as if you could know what a Justice of the Peace was by knowing from a dictionary what these fine words mean.

In this book, I try to understand things in political terms. But as is stressed in the first chapter, this itself requires a 'political' criticism of the tendency to locate 'the political' in the hands of the institutions, and especially the state, that are officially promulgated as the proper sphere of politics. Far from being the sole routes of politics' the 'proper channels' themselves exist in political competition with other paths. What I mean to bring out, then, in emphasising the 'political' dimension of the state, law, morality and production, is the 'conflict of forces' in terms of which these institutions and activities have to be understood. And to such conflict there is no special solving agency. Rather the claims of special agencies to regulate, manage or control conflict are best seen as themselves salvoes in that conflict, and then it may be asked whether such agencies may not be perpetuating the evils they claim to suppress.

CHAPTER 1

PHILOSOPHICAL STATISM

The Logic of Loyalty

Academic political philosophers generally take it for granted that their duty and privilege is to justify 'the state'. Impressing us with 'the state's' *a priori* achievements: order, liberty, peace, welfare, they seldom encumber their court-portraits with the more empirical trappings of nation-states, lest an awareness of chaos, oppression, war, corruption, exploitation, should dim our respect and gratitude. For academic as for governmental purposes, it seems, 'the state' is by definition its people's redeemer, and history is the exception which proves the rule. The English Idealists, such as Bernard Bosanquet in *The Philosophical Theory of the State*, 1923 used to say that they were speaking of the state only in so far as it matched its Idea. But Bosanquet wrote as if this match could be assumed - as if, by its very nature, the state, unlike the state's subjects, were what it is meant to be. Today, despite the decline of official Idealism, this conflation continues.

In *The Origin of the Family, Private Property and the State*, Engels wrote:

> As the state arose from the need to hold class antagonisms in check, but as it arose, at the same time, in the midst of a conflict of those classes, it is as a rule, the state of the most powerful, economically dominant class, which, through the medium of the state, becomes also the politically dominant class, and thus acquires new means of holding down and exploiting the oppressed class.

Engels was trying to give a true account of the nature and historical development of the state. If he is anything like right, much of the priestly writing of our political philosophers has to be seen as pious nonsense. But the possibility of confronting Engels' perspective in its own

realistic terms is blocked off by the philosophical framework
of the orthodox practitioners: their enquiry is 'normative',
not 'factual', 'conceptual', not 'empirical', into 'principles'
rather than 'practices'. What these dichotomies mask is
activity of theoretical sublimation in which the state gets
presented as the embodiment of concepts and principles; as,
like the Church of the apologists, an ideal entity. Perhaps,
however, the state is not the sort of thing which lends itself to
following norms, and perhaps the official concepts distort
reality. And in any case it is ironic that it is a 'realistic'
account of the shortcomings of human nature that standardly
launches the philosophical text's ascent to political heaven.
Thus, our Sunday School academics teach us that the
ordinary man's arbitrariness requires the state's impartiality:
the ordinary man's selfishness requires the state's justice; the
ordinary man's wilfulness requires the state's policing; the
ordinary man's fallibility requires the state's judgment. So,
unjustly enough to the ordinary man, the state gets singled
out for special treatment, the gap between would-be
psychological realism and full-blown political idealism
serving to justify the hierarchical gap between state and
people, authority and subject. 'For reasons of state', states
practise the very crimes it is their supposed purpose to
prevent, and are helped to do so by staffs of philosophical
sanctifiers.

To present politics as above politics shows a certain
wisdom in political advertising. To present the state as above
the shortcomings of human social life, as is in fact their
solution, shows a certain conceptual daring. To present the
political forms which have attained dominance only in
comparatively recent times as necessities of human thought
shows a certain preemptive panache. Let us sample this loyal
logic.

First-person Pluralism

Our attitude to authority is really ambivalent. When we are
drawn into war, we grant the authority and power necessary for
the exigencies of the situation; and this has involved the
extension of the arm of government into many fields previously
considered outside its reach. Even restrictions on the freedom

of the press and freedom of speech... are accepted and the
authority is not felt to be oppressive. In many peacetime
enterprises it is not regarded as an interference when we want
to get things done, for example, about seaports, roadways or
river systems that serve several states or cities. Whenever we
must break through the habits of jealousy and self-interest and
a previously demonstrated inability to agree and get on with
needed business, an authority is proposed for its obvious
benefits, and the name 'authority' is readily employed in
designating any such useful agency. That authority which
secures for us some particular public good is then entirely
acceptable. (Presidential Address by Professor Charles
Hendel to the Association of American Legal and Political
Philosophy, printed in *Nomos,* 1958)

Hendel is here asking his readers to see the state as a
bureau for managing society's affairs. Its authority appears
unproblematic: 'we' want to get something done, only the
state can do it, so 'we' duly authorise it to take the 'necessary'
steps. And so 'we', 'the public', ordinary decent folk that we
are, happily submit ourselves to conscription, censorship,
compulsory purchases and demolitions, rather as a patient
submits to having his appendix out. Hendel says 'we' cannot
agree, but presents the disagreement as unproblematic, as a
function of such disagreeable things as 'self-interest' and
'jealousy', not to mention 'inabilty to agree'. And so, far
from massive state intervention reflecting deep splits and
conflicts in society, far from the state acting on behalf of some
forces against others, this growth of coercive power is seen as
something 'we' all ask for. Thus, devoid of 'selfish habits' of
its own, the state is called in by 'us' for its 'obvious benefits'.

Waterloo and the playing-fields of Eton

Of course there are plenty of good reasons for accepting
authority in general (though they may not always apply in
particular). We are often in a situation where it is more
important to accept an umpire's judgement rather than insist
on our own. When little boys play cricket without an umpire,
they spend more time arguing than playing cricket. Cricket is a
better game if everyone agrees to accept an umpire's decision
instead of insisting on his own judgement (however impartial)
every time the ball hits the batsman's pads. Again there are

plenty of good reasons for accepting leadership. An army will usually do better with bad generals than with no generals at all. We accept authority because most social enterprises would be hopeless without it. Nevertheless it is the enterprise that counts; the authority is conditional on the way it promotes or preserves it. (S.I. Benn and R.S. Peters, *Social Principles and the Democratic State,* London 1959, p.329)

Now, of course there are plenty of good reasons for *not* accepting authority in general (though they might not apply in particular). Let us leave aside the fact that little boys often seem to get on very well umpiring their own games. Let us leave aside that an army's doing well for its chiefs is frequently a matter of indifference to its rank-and-file members. Into the amorphous bag of 'authority-in-general', the rule of the general authoritarian, Benn and Peters have packed the uniforms of two incompatible models of political authority. Umpires rule games whose rules are generally laid down in advance to give each side an even chance and are accepted in advance by the players as the basis of the game. So when Benn and Peters say that 'government is in the position of an umpire' (*Principles*, p. 275) they are presenting the state-authorised proper channels as analogous to the rules of a game. Hence, not only are 'all sides' legitimated (providing they have paid their entry fee), the state's role is seen as that of an impartial arbitrator among equals, aloof from the struggle. The 'authority-in-general' of the general is a different matter, and a more appropriate model for the interventionist state in pursuit of substantial 'national goals'. No umpire, the general, as leader, has a job to do - to win; and he must take such steps as are necessary in the deployment of troops, weapons and support. Thus military authoritarianism can appear to the well-drilled mind as a merely technical kind of thing, providing another 'apolitical' model of the state. By focusing our minds on the need to defeat the enemy without, the image destracts us from the forces battling within society.

The Book of Necessary Beings

J. R. Lucas tells us on page 1 of his *Principles of Politics* (Oxford, 1966) that 'we can see how political institutions depend on the nature of men constituting political communities'. (For the nature of women, see Mr. Lucas' 'Because you are a woman', *Philosophy,* April 1973.) Indeed,

> ... it is because human nature is as we have described it and in particular, because of the fallibility of human judgement, that we need to have, and can have, the methods of settling disputes that we actually do have. (p.13)

Lucas goes further: not only do English political forms answer the needs of human nature, they are needed by logic itself:

> ... it is logically necessary for people to be able to recognise 'Authority' and give way to it if they are to be members of a community at all and not outlaws. If a man involved in a dispute with his neighbour were not able to call a policeman, unable to find a magistrate to summon his neighbour to appear, unable to invoke the protection of a king, because there was no means of telling policemen, magistrates or kings apart from other folk, then there would be no way of settling the dispute... and every encounter or dispute would end in a resort to violence. (pp. 14-15)

How much bloody history could have been avoided had men appreciated some simple demands of reason! But then, states are prone to get into violent disputes and disagreements — often ending in imprisonment or death — not only with their own 'neighbours', but with those officially under their 'protection'. Does logic necessitate a Still Higher Authority to resolve such disputes? On the other hand there is evidence that social life can go on and disputes can be peacefully settled in the absence of policemen, magistrates and kings - no doubt a further tribute to men's limited capacity to appreciate their logical limitations. Lucas demonstrates further powers of the *a priori*: 'So, too, the rule of precedence is not just a quirk of Anglo-Saxon common law but again a logical necessity'. (p. 18) - as if acceptance of past judgements as a basis for present ones was a tribute not to conservatism but to logic. Again: '... judges are necessary because of the fallibility of human judgement' (p. 19) - as if this very fallibility should not lead us to question the position of the popes of the judiciary.

Respect for Persons; Disrespect for Personnel

> The basis for self-esteem in a just society is not then one's income share but the publicly affirmed distribution of fundamental rights and liberties. And this distribution being equal, every one has a similar and secure status when they meet to conduct the common affairs of the wider society... When it is the position of equal citizenship that answers to the need for status, the precedence of equal liberties becomes all the more necessary. Having chosen a conception of justice that seeks to eliminate the relative economic and social advantages as supports for men's self-confidence, it is essential that the priority of liberty be firmly maintained... Thus the best solution is to support the primary good of self-respect as far as possible by the assignment of the basic liberties that can be made equal, defining the same status for all... distributive justice... justice in the relative share of material means, is relegated to a subordinate place... While these principles permit inequalities in return for contributions that are for the benefit of all, the precedence of liberty entails equality in the social bases of esteem. (John Rawls, *A Theory of Justice*, Harvard, 1971, pp. 545-6)

Rawls is saying that it is our position as equal citizens, guaranteed by civil liberty, that is basic to our self respect and hence our happiness. Thus he espouses a dualism in the principles of justice, giving primacy to 'political' liberty and relegating 'socio-economic' position to secondary importance. Since the basic good of self respect *should* depend, he claims, on status as citizen, not on position in the economy, a just society may well be one with great inequality in its economic organisation, just as long as this inequality leaves the 'worst off' better off than they would be under other systems - a claim made for capitalism by its major proponents from Adam Smith to Milton Friedman.

Thus it is in their place in the state that people find their highest contentment. Rawls admits that wealth affects people's ability to exercise citizenship rights, but preserves the basic dualism of his theory with the idea that the effect of this wealth is not on liberty as such (political), but on the 'worth of liberty' (economic), (p. 204). So, while the millionaire and the pauper may be equally free to fly to Washington each week to help 'conduct the common affairs of the wider society', it turns out that the pauper's freedom is not 'worth' much. Still, his self-respect as citizen should not be impaired. Rawls systematically underplays the role of the economy in the state and in people's control over it. But what constitutes Rawls' statism is his overall elevation of state life to the centre of human life and his complementary relegation of 'the economy', the major locus of people's daily lives, to a peripheral place in his scheme of things. And with that goes a failure to see the 'political' character of hierarchies of power and authority within the organisation of production itself; as if daily questions of production and consumption did not raise issues of 'self-respect', 'citizenship' and 'liberty'. It is as if the requirements of economic justice could be dealt with by Social Security.

Logically Proper Channels

These philosophers, then, in different ways, offer *a priori* glorifications of state authority. They see the state as the sacred light in a profane society, as a kind of transcendental ego of society, uniting and regulating the chaotic impulses of society's empirical self, as if it operated at a different level of casuality from what it oversees. Such statism, of course, nurtures itself on an equally *a priori* individualism, a view of human beings as fundamentally private, selfish, infinitely demanding and rather unreasonable. Lacking internal principles of mutual organisation, human passions and human individuals require the organisation they need to come from outside and above - hence the need for that holy trinity: Morality, Religion and The State. Marx suggested a more mundane role for the state in his account of the development of the French nation-state:

> Every *common* interest was straightway severed from society, counterposed to it as a higher, *general* interest, snatched from the activity of society's members themselves and made an object of government activity; from a bridge, a schoolhouse and the communal property of a village community to the railways, the national wealth and the National University of France. (*Selected works of Marx and Engels,* Moscow, 1962, Vol 1, p. 333)

As Marx brings out here, the duality of state and society

and the atomisation of social life, far from being the justification of state supremacy, is in large measure itself a function of state rule. The state claims a monopoly of political life, and this claim is contested. But our philosophers oblige, presenting state monopoly not only as justified, but as a conceptual given. Politics, it seems, just *is* the state's business. A.M. Quinton writes, for example: 'The central concept of political science is that of the state,' (Editorial Introduction to *Oxford Readings in Political Philosophy,* 1967, p. 3). And according to Professor D.D. Raphael: 'the political is whatever concerns the state' (*Problems of Political Philosophy* Macmillan, 1976, p. 27) - so the state makes water holy just by brewing its afternoon tea. The view is received and standard, and has a long and deeply rooted history; it focuses on the state as the one locus of politics. Our political philosophers, thinking of the state as a pure agency, seldom ask what it is; sometimes they equate it with the 'government', sometimes they content themselves with gestures in the direction of parliamentary buildings or courtrooms. In any case, the state is seen as a special institution, of-but-above society and, (to the necessary extent,) regulating it. And this institution and its activities are supposed to be what politics and political philosophy are about.

So, not only is the state-institution a requirement of human reason, it has politics all to itself by definition. A curious paradox: political philosophers, like statesmen themselves, have contrived to elevate the state above politics with one hand while putting the masses below politics with the other. What this amounts to is the presentation of a central empirical fact of modern social existence, the relative monopolisation of social authority by the nation-state institution, in the form of a philosophical category. By attributing social organisation *a priori* to the state, conceived of as that-which-organises-us, as the 'internal nominative' of politics, statist philosophy makes it seem that politics is the state's domain by logical necessity. Hence philosophical sanctification is given to a de-politicisation of everyday social life, to its confinement in production and consumption channels cut and defined from above; and a substantial governmental élitism is passed off as the formal fruit of Reason.

'Scientific' State-worship

If the positivist taboo on overt advocacy has forced philosophers' values and outlooks to lurk behind 'analysis', the schools of 'political science' have been adept at disguising their pieties as hard fact.

Consider the Weberian tradition, and especially Weber's own 'definition' of the state as:

> ... A human community that (successfully) claims the monopoly of the legitimate use of force within a given territory... The state is considered the sole source of the 'right' to use violence. ('Politics as a Vocation' in *From Max Weber, edited by Gerth and Mills,* Routledge and Kegan Paul, 1948, p. 78)

Note that Weber says 'legitimate', so that, to the claim that there are individuals, groups and forces within territories that break and even contest, with more or less success, this 'monopoly', it would be replied that their force and violence are not 'legitimate', the state's are. What is to be made of this? In J.N. Figgis's *Political Theory from Gerson to Grotius,* (Cambridge 1907) it is made very clear that in those times the state very much shared the accepted control of force with other institutions, most obviously the church, the guilds and the family. Perhaps these states were not 'states' in the full modern sense? But we must remember that even today the state draws on other social institutions as sources for its 'legitimacy' and implicity recognises its limited sovereignty. Think of parental rights to punish children and the way corporal punishment in state schools is 'legitimated' in terms of the 'normal parent'. Think of the way in which governments pretend to 'manage society' on the model of a business enterprise, and of the degree of power more or less autonomously exercised by capitalist companies, whether or not they use private police in pursuing their normal affairs. Think of the right to carry guns in the U.S.A., a right treasured as more basic by its advocates than any congressional or court decision. Think of class-violence, of battles against industrial laws. The state's authority, its 'legitimate monopoly', is limited, partial, and a matter of perpetual contestation, and Weber simply buries this in an *a priori* way. And so, keeping with the finest traditions of state self-certification, the 'legitimacy' of the modern state boils down to the demand of the state to be obeyed. This applies to H.V. Wiseman's definition of the political in his *Politics: The Master Science*, Routlege, 1969:

> Politics is a way of getting things done governmentally (p. 12).

> Political organisation differs from economical, social, religious and other organisations in that conflict over ends and means within and among such organisations cannot be resolved in ways binding on all members of society without the participation of the political organisation. As Robert A. Dahl (Modern Political Analysis) reminds us, the state or government must 'successfully uphold a claim to the exclusive regulation of legitimate use of physical force in enforcing its rule within a given territorial area.(pp. 3-4)

Now, 'legitimate' here can again mean little more than state-approved, and Wiseman and Dahl's 'must' can be little more than a statist demand posed as a requirement of logic. Wiseman's definitions seem to presuppose that state certification and enforcement is a necessary condition of social life's continuing, as though the degree of accommodation that does occur among complex and conflicting forces in society could occur only if it were 'bound' to occur by a higher power; and as though the state did in any case keep society under control. But 'conflict over ends and means' commonly occurs between state institutions and other institutions, and, apparently in defiance of logic, the state is frequently 'bound' to step down. In the real world, then, state-sovereignty, far from being a necessary fact, is itself politically contested, a fact buried by the analytic authoritarianism of the establishment theorists. David Easton, armed with 'systems theory' - 'political theory unlike anything that preceded it in the last two thousand years' (*Varieties of Political Theory*, Prentice Hall, 1966, p. 1) identifies the 'political system' not as a structure of interacting forces, but with the state itself, as regulator of those forces, so that the 'political system' regulates society, through its 'outputs' to other 'systems', thereby setting in train a 'feedback loop' which

> ... consists of the production of outputs by the authorities, a response by the members of the society to these outputs, the communication of information about this response to the authorities, and finally possible succeeding action by the authorities. (Easton, p. 152)

This way of thinking evidently suits the statesmen: when Scottish miners' leader Mick McGahey announced in 1974 that miners would appeal to troops not to break the miners' strike, ministers Harold Wilson and James Callaghan rounded on him to mind his own business and leave politics to the elected politicians. It seems our theorists want us to see the propriety of these channels as a logical one, and to confine our inputs to the ballot box.

The Statist Conception of Politics

If the term 'politics' is restricted to activities centring on state authorities, it is difficult to see how anyone can go on seeing politics as a 'categorial', that is basic, universal and distinctive dimension of human life, difficult, therefore, to see that there might be a proper field of political philosophy at all, as distinct from a 'second order' adjunct to departments of social administration ('Political Science'). After all, the state-institution as we understand it has evolved contingently and historically and in intimate relation to the very mundane development of capitalism and nationalism. The basic 'problems of politics', moreover, problems of justice, order, freedom, welfare, are problems which are not only found at all levels of human existence: they are problems which, even at the level at which the state defines them, seem largely over the state's head. In the capitalist countries of the West, forms of work, incomes, prices of consumer goods and of labour, technological development, employment and population patterns, crime and violence - indeed the greater part of what shapes people's ways of living - are only partially subject to the control of state 'policy'.

Indeed, it would appear that the state's principal and desperate struggle at this time is to keep itself in business by trying to keep this wider system in operation; so it is only in a manner of speaking that we should speak of the 'government' at all. Despite our states, and in many respects because of them, social life is much more 'anarchic' than political philosophy conceives. Yet our theorists continue to write as if the state is that-which-keeps-order-in-the-world. The Argument from Design lives on.

The Political and the Unpolitical

Conceptual deference is not of course peculiar to politics: higher entities abound in all areas of thought: theology has 'God', psychology has 'the self' and sociology has 'society'. And 'philosophy of education' treats the state school as the one locus of education. Like the state, and unlike God or the immortal soul, the school is real enough. What is mythical is its presentation as being, essentially and specifically, that-which-educates. It becomes difficult, then, for a student even to entertain the proposition that such institutions, far from resolving the problems of freedom and reason in society, are themselves an important part of the political and educational problem. If, as R.S. Peters says, it is only in a stretched sense that a visit to a brothel could be said to be 'an education' *(Ethics and Education)*, it is certainly only in a cramped sense that an education is gained from the schools so dutifully rationalised in contemporary 'philosophy of education'.

But even our protected conceptual protectors cannot freeze concepts forever, and the whole idea of logically proper channels of political life is in question. People are acting outside the officially marked zones and are conscious of the 'political' nature of what they are doing. Young men and women are making schools and families centres of direct political struggle, and workers are overcoming the phobic notion that industrial struggle and political struggle are separate departments to be controlled by separate department heads. Our political monopolists are having increasing difficulty in maintaining the impression that politics is their proprietary right, to be conducted in their proprietary way. And since statism involves the promulgation of certain political manners as well as the appropriation of certain political matters, the liberation of politics from the state involves political practices appropriate to issues with which the state, with the best will in the world, can hardly deal.

This breakthrough is not universal, nor is it stable. A statist conception of politics is by no means confined to defenders of the *status quo* who both uphold statist politics and confine the notion of politics to the state. Statism obviously pervades the thinking of those Stalino-Marxists for whom revolution consists in replacing capitalism with state 'socialism'. Their antithesis is all those anarchists and libertarians who turn bourgeois political ideology directly on its head and deride 'politics' as the essentially manipulative practice of power-mongering 'politicians' and 'politicos', failing thereby to develop a serious libertarian politics. The anarchist who says he is against 'politics' is thus as much in the grip of a statist conception of politics as is the Bolshevik who scorns his 'apoliticality'. By falling for this compartmentalising conceptual scheme, moreover, both contribute to the political withdrawal and consent that passes for 'apoliticality'.

Common to both these left orientations, then, are central elements of the conventional statist ideology and in particular the idea that politics is not a dimension of everyday life activity. But to the extent that radicals respect this dualism, this separation of politics and confinement of it to the charge of a special entity, they are hampering the breakdown of social divisions. Either they will, in the name of 'scientific politics', reduce struggle in key political areas - schools, factories, families, communities - to mere instruments of what is in effect a militarist strategy for a smash-and-grab raid on the bourgeois state apparatus, or, at the other extreme, they will, in the name of 'anti-political' purity, be active where they are, but inconsequentially, often at the level of intermittent theatre politics. In either case the ready-made packaging of 'the political' and 'the non-political' preempts exploration of the actual political relations of conflict and support among institutions. In either case the understanding is held up of the balance and movement of political forces, making it more difficult to work out priorities of political struggle. We are seeing political awareness break out all over the place, including the bedroom; it would be wise to break out of ideologies inhibiting us from a rich and full political life.

It is possible to identify politics with state-focused activity and then to go on and, within those terms, scorn or belittle it. This is common in all sorts of dimensions of social experience. Some people identify art or culture or education or morality with very special activities going on at special times in special places, and then advocate a 'rejection' of such activities as inherently alienated, élitist or peripheral. Such positions can be quite consistent but they involve those who hold them in making fairly arbitrary disjunctions. And they encourage a blindness to the presence of what I should want to call 'political', 'artistic', 'cultural' or 'educational' activities, alive as every-day realities, as well as to the scandal of their scarcity and poverty. If, for example, you confine your idea of what is artistic to the work of 'artists', not only do you blind yourself to such things as people's gardens, but you legitimise the everyday ugliness and squalor with which the specialists of modern capitalism surround our sense-organs. Similarly, if you accept the established notion of what is political, you blind yourself to the everyday reality of 'political' struggle and also legitimise the dominant fact of pervasive passivity that is the modern state's gift to everyday life.

Statism, Ancient and Modern

Epicurus, revolting against the idea that the city-state was the institution fundamental to the good life, characterised his own advocacy of amicable communalism as 'anti-political'. And this bears witness to the ancient charter that is possessed by the statist conception of politics. Plato, by setting up the 'art of rule' as a specialism in *The Republic* and by conse-crating 'temperance' as knowing the need for such rule, has a lot to answer for. But he was to urge that the differences

between 'political' rule and other levels of rule, for example,
over slaves or over the household, were differences of scale,
not of kind:

> *Eleatic Stranger:* One science covers all these several spheres
> and we will not quarrel with a man who prefers any one of the
> particular names for it; he can call it royal science, political
> science or the science of household management.
> *Socrates:* It makes no difference (The Statesman, 259c)

And in *The Republic,* of course, he had gone further and
presented intra-psychic life, with its three 'parts', in the terms
of·a political model, the attempt being vitiated more by the
inadequacies of his hierarchial and technocratic model of
politics than by any fundamental incoherence in the idea of a
political model of psychology.

Aristotle, more conventional, took Plato to task for
denying that there was a difference in kind between the
statesman and the master of house or business (*Politics*
Book 1). But while insisting on the specific essence of
'politics' against Plato's 'reductionism', all he could say was
that politics aims at the Highest Good, the assumption being
that public life in the Greek city-state realised this end. Now
the Greek *polis,* as every good student knows, cannot simply
be translated by 'state' in our modern sense. It is important to
stress, however, against any tendency to think of Athens as
some sort of ideal community, not only that membership of
the 'political community' was narrowly restricted, but that so
too was the area of life thought worth dignifying as 'political'.
Thus, even then, 'politics' conventionally picked out a circumscribed field of ruling-class concern. Slavery was presented by Aristotle, for example, not as itself a political fact, but
as a precondition of political life. And the household
'economy' was treated as a more or less autonomous sub-
political entity. Such is Plato's unconcern with production
that he almost ignores it, leaving it to those best equipped to
govern such things. So 'politics' is something special - and
Hannah Arendt, with her characteristic love of the ancient
ways, criticises the post-Athenean 'confusion' of polity,
society and economy, and of public and private life, and
criticises the Roman and Mediaeval translation of Aristotle's

zoon politikon ('political animal') as *animal socialis* ('social animal'), (*The Human Condition,* Chapter 3). Ironically, W.G. Runciman, while referring to Arendt's discussion as if it were authoritative, does not notice that he is contradicting her when he writes:

> ... a distinction between the political and the social is still recent in the history of ideas. (*Social Science and Political Theory* Cambridge, p.22)

Statism·could hardly flourish in the Middle Ages, since secular authority was not emancipated from the maternal clutches of The Church. Indeed, to the inspiration of the 'pluralist' proponents of Guild Socialism, such as G.D.H. Cole, this was a time in which the interaction of relatively independent institutions, church, town, guild, was not only a fact of life, but was recognised in ideological debates over the proper frame-work of social life. That the movement towards philosophical statism, in the form of 'sovereignty' theory, was itself an agent of the movement to the post-Renaissance absolute state emerges in Figgis's *From Gerson to Grotius*. What also emerges is the power of the notion of 'the individual' as detached from social networks and held in relation with others only by fear either of God or of the state. Thus did the rising state clothe itself with what it stripped from ways of social life that had gone on independently, and proceed to set itself up as our saviour from nakedness. Thus did 'sovereignty', the ideology of the early modern state, become the central notion which continues to haunt the pages of more contemporary apologists for more contemporary powers-that-be.

Politics as Superstructure: Marx

But statist conceptions have dominated radical thought as well. The outcome of the French Revolution, with its project of a 'political', that is, state, solution to social antagonisms and injustices, provoked among radical theorists what was expressed as a revulsion from politics. This took one form in the 'anti-political' technocratism of Saint-Simon, Comte and the 'positivists'. And the later anarchist movement clearly articulated its anti-statism as 'anti-political'. Bakunin, though here writing in 1870, (precisely to attack Marx's 'statism' in the sense of his advocacy of state-socialism), exemplifies a well established 'anti-political' tradition:

> ...the workers of Germany and not their leaders will finish by joining us in order to smash these prisons of peoples that are called states and to condemn politics which is indeed nothing but the art of dominating and fleecing the masses. (*Marxism, Freedom and the state*, Freedom Press, U.K., 1950, p.44)

Sorel, in *Reflections on Violence* (1907), counterposes the 'anti-political' syndicalist form of struggle to the 'political' social-democrat form in which, he says, 'the politicians' would seek to climb on the backs of the workers' grass-roots movement in order to grab state power for themselves (see especially chapters 4 and 5 of *Reflections on Violence*). What the anarchists were insisting was that the state could not be seen simply as an obedient organ of class rule; that it had its own structure and its own way of working which would catch up any movements that sought to achieve social liberation through it. Thus, for example, the abolition of private capitalism in no way guarantees the collapse of the state and hence in no way guarantees the collapse of oppression and exploitation in society.

Now, in their struggle with the Proudhonists and Bakunin-ites, Marx and Engels accepted the terms in which the latter presented their attack on Marxist 'politicians'. Engels, for example, spoke of Bakunin's 'complete abstention from all politics' (Letter from Engels to Cuno, 24 January, 1872, *Marx and Engels, Selected Works*, Volume 2, p. 468). Marx and Engels, and Lenin too, fairly consistently identified politics, in capitalist society at least, with activity centring on the state; whether state activity itself or activity oriented towards legislative change, or the revolutionary capture of state power. And this despite the radical impact that the Paris Commune had on Marx's thought. For Marx, then, 'economic' struggles are not inherently political:

> For instance, the attempt of workers in a particular factory or even a particular trade to force a shorter working day out of the individual capitalists by strikes etc. is a purely economic movement. On the other hand, the movement to force an

eight-hour day *law* is a political movement. (Marx to Bolte, 1871. Selected Works, Vol II, p. 467).

Politics as Alienation

Marx sees politics as a phenomenon of the epochs of oppression, not as a permanent category of social life. He wrote that in communist society, 'when state power disappears and governmental functions are transformed into simple administrative functions... there will no longer be any state in the present political sense of the word' ('The alleged splits in the International', 1872, and 'Marx on Bakunin', 1875, most readily available in David McLennan's *The Thought of Karl Marx,* Macmillan, 1971, (pp. l94-5). That Marx puts it this way, rather than saying that there will be no politics in the present *statist* sense, is significant and not merely a verbal matter. For it forms the linguistic expression of the utopian idea that social authority could be merely 'administrative' and non-political, a latent managerialism made explicit in Engels 'On Authority' and now enshrined in the humanist fascism that passes for Soviet political theory. What Marx's formulation excludes, then, is the question of the kind of democratic political life that would be the mark of a real communist society.

Marx's analysis of capitalism stresses the 'superstructural' place of politics and of the state as an organ of class rule. Thus politics becomes seen as one historical *form* or means of class struggle, more or less central according to circumstances. In a sense, then, Marx did not propose a 'materialistic' account of politics, and tended to contrast 'material' forces with their more or less obscuring politico-spiritual manifestations. Thus 'political' power is regularly contrasted in the Marxist literature with 'social' or 'economic' power, while 'political' freedom and equality are said to conceal 'social' oppression and inequality. Now obviously the base-superstructure notion does not entail a statist conception of politics. But by stressing the official, legalistic, more or less superficial forms of politics, statism certainly helps a base-superstructure framework. This can emerge clearly only in the process of trying to show how, if we break from the statist framework of politics, we are naturally led to locate politics in the depths of 'concrete material life', in a way that represents a more radical thrust implicit in Marxism. Meanwhile, it is Marx's statism of form and later of substance that will concern us.

In Marx's early anarchistic thinking, politics, like religion, is an alienated and 'abstract domain', a partial, mystifying and destructive expression of man's social essence. In 'On the Jewish Question', the limitations of 'political emancipation' equated with civil rights, are exposed:

> Only when the actual individual man has taken back into himself the abstract citizen and in his everyday life, his individual work and his individual relationships, has become a species-being, only when he has recognised his powers as social powers, so that social power is no longer separated from him as political power, only then is human emancipation complete.
> (*Writings of the Young Marx on Philosophy and Society,* edited by C.D. Easton and K.H. Guddat, Doubleday, 1967)

The position is, if anything, even more clearly put in Marx's criticism of Arnold Ruge: 'The King of Prussia and Social Reform', a superb attack on statist panaceas, which should disturb many Marxist-Leninist-Trotskyists today:

> ... The more powerful the state and hence the more political a country is, the less it is inclined to seek the basis and seek the general principle of social ills in the principle of the state itself, thus in the existing order of society of which the state is the active, self-conscious and official expression. Political thought is political precisely because it takes place within the bounds of politics. The more acute and vigorous it is the more incapable it is of comprehending social ills. (Easton and Guddat, p. 350)

> ... We have seen that a social revolution involves the standpoint of the whole because it is a protest of man against dehumanised life, even if it occurs in only one factory district, because it proceeds from the standpoint of the single actual individual, because the community against whose separation from himself the individual reacts, is the true community of man, human existence. The political soul of a revolution on the other hand consists in the tendency of politically uninfluential classes to end their isolation from the state and from power. Its standpoint is that of the state, an abstract whole, which exists only through separation from actual life and which is unthinkable without the organised antithesis between the

universal idea and the individual existence of man. Hence a
revolution of the political soul also organises, in accordance
with the narrow and split nature of this soul, a ruling group at
society's expense. (Easton and Guddat, pp. 350, 356)

'Politics', then, equated with state-focused activity, merely
expresses, disguises and perpetuates the 'social' ills it
purports to cure, ills which Marx says must have a 'social'
solution. However, since he places such things as 'power' and
conflict in the enemy camp of 'politics', we are left at this
stage with little more than a wistful dream.

From his earlier period Marx tends to present politics not
only as a partial but as a surface feature ('expression') of
bourgeois society. 'Society' or later 'the capitalist economy'
gets to be represented as more or less autonomous in its
dynamics, clearly visible beneath its political-ideological
garments in all its ugliness. Thus the famous passage in the
Communist Manifesto:

> The bourgeoisie, whenever it has got the upper hand, has put
> an end to all feudal, idyllic, patriarchial relations. It has
> pitilessly torn aside the motely feudal ties that bound man to his
> 'natural superiors' and has left no other nexus between man
> and man than naked self-interest, than callous 'cash-payment'.
> It has drowned the most heavenly ecstasies of religious fervour,
> of chivalrous enthusiasm, of philistine sentimentalism, in the
> icy water of egoistical calculation. It has resolved personal
> worth into exchange value, and in place of numberless
> indefeasible chartered freedoms, has set up that single
> unconscionable freedom - Free Trade. In one word, for
> exploitation veiled by religious and political illusion it has
> substituted shameless direct brutal exploitation... (*Selected
> Works*, Vol. I, Moscow, p.36)

In *Capital,* Marx emphasises the peripheral place of
'politics', now identified with state force, in capitalist
society's dynamics:

> ... the dull compulsion of economic relations completes the
> subjection of the labourer to the capitalist. Direct force,
> outside economic conditions, is of course still used, but only
> exceptionally. In the ordinary run of things, the labourer can
> be left to 'the natural laws of production', that is to his
> dependence on capital, a dependence springing from and

guaranteed in perpetuity by the conditions of production
themselves. (Vol 1, Chapter 28, Moscow edition p. 137)

It is at the level of 'the economy', then, that capitalist
society maintains itself while digging its own grave through
'the falling rate of profit'. The state is cast into the role,
meanwhile, of nightwatchman. But, at capitalism's 'rosy
dawn' the state, according to Marx in *Capital,* had played the
central and vital role as 'midwife', since capitalism's
existence 'presupposed' laws whereby 'the agricultural
people were first turned into vagabonds and then whipped,
branded, tortured by laws grotesquely terrible into the
discipline necessary for the wage system'. So Marx
emphasises the protracted battle for control, for power, for
discipline, whose issue was the capitalist society of *Capital,*
and writes as if, that battle having been won, it is at the level
of economics, of 'the labour theory of value' for example,
that we are to understand the continuing and developing
exploitation of capitalist society proper. But, then, having
been cast into a secondary role for the playing through of
capitalism's tragedy, politics abruptly re-occupies the centre
of the stage at its revolutionary denoument, with wholesale
'nationalisation' under the 'dictatorship of the proletariat',
whose exercise is spelled out in the Communist Manifesto in
wholly statist terms. Certainly the Paris Commune forced
Marx to recognise that 'the working class cannot simply lay
hold of the ready-made state machinery and wield it for its
own purposes' and notes that the communards' plan was that
'the commune was to be the political form of even the
smallest country hamlet' *(The Civil War in France, Selected
Works*, Moscow, Vol. 1, p. 520). But, as the First International battles with Bakunin display, these insights did not
issue in any fundamental shift of theory, either of the state or
of politics in general; they remain *ad hoc* modifications within the Marxian corpus, which can be linked to other writings
to constitute an undercurrent which radically conflicts with
the 'economism' that undeniably dominates Marx's work.
Is politics secondary in capitalist society, to become crucial in
its overthrow? Clearly, if what is at issue here is principally
Marx's dominant conception of what politics is, such a

question cannot be confronted in a simple empirical way. But without even breaking from the conventional understanding of politics that Marx was operating with, it is possible to see that the ways in which the capitalist order diverges from the *Communist Manifesto* presentation are too many and too important to be thought of as aberrations or survivals.

Accepting a crude equation of state agency and political agency, and accepting the 'economists" propaganda about a self-regulating market society, Marx and Engels presented society as abandoned to a thinly disguised economic determination. It then appears anomalous that the British state, for example, developed precisely in capitalism's nineteenth-century heyday, penetrating not only heavy industry but all areas of social life. The state police force emerged to control the working class, whole sections of which threatened precisely not to be subjected to the 'dull compulsion' of market forces. Nor was this police force simply a brute coercive power. From the very beginning it orientated itself towards winning the support of the 'honest public' and towards enforcing an ideological isolation on 'society's enemies'. Isolation, separation, 'special treatment', were the watchwords of the burgeoning asylums, prisons, 'educational institutions'. The organisation of work itself was no 'merely economic' matter: the technology of the Industrial Revolution and the wage system itself having as much to do with the imposition of control over the actions of workers and over the products of their labours as with 'efficiency' conceived in some apolitical sense. But to stress these things, to stress the centrality of questions of control and to emphasise the place of 'culture', is already to strain the narrowly conceived notion of politics that Marx shared with the ideologues of the *status quo* he was fighting - is to think in terms of a 'political order'. In this wider context, we can discuss the political character and importance of the family institution, the school, and of the trade unions whose compensatory respectability and competitive status-mongering countervailed their usually recognised character as organs of class struggle. And so for newspapers, literature, and the churches. Certainly, Engels especially, wrote about these institutions and their changes, but

overwhelmingly in 'economistic' terms — he ignored, for
example, in *The Origins of the Family, Private Property and
the State,* the political importance of the family, not only in
the bourgeoisie but in the working class, where the family as
we know it was developing, not only as a defence against
bourgeois domination at work, but, contradictorily, as a
vehicle of bourgeois domination, as a principal organ for
reproducing class membership, helping to mould and force
individual men and women into their work-roles. Engels, on
the other hand, thought the monogamous family unit almost
extinct among the proletarians, since its function was the
passing on of property and the proletariat had no property
to pass on.

In short, even with regard to their own time, it is arguable
that Marx and Engels hugely underrated the capitalist
political order's mode of preserving the sheer existence of a
proletarian productive force through the prolonged periods
of transformation, war, crisis and recession that have marked
capitalist society since its birth. Despite their eye for politics,
seen most clearly in their analyses of French and German
struggles rather than in their writings on Britain, Marx and
Engels' way of thinking pushed them into seeing the political
structure of capitalist society as a surface feature of an order
whose depths could only be plumbed by Economic Science.

Writing at a time when according to Marx political
ideology was in the process of annihilation, Edmund Burke
was able to present clearly and prophetically what classical
Marxism has been constitutionally tempted to lay down. He
points, not to the conscious politicking of the bourgeosie's
executive committee, but to the deep structural network that
props up, conceals and partially constitutes domination and
exploitation:

> ...Good order is the foundation of all good things. To be able to
> acquire, the people, without being servile, must be tractable
> and obedient. The magistrate must have his reverence, the
> laws their authority. The body of the people must not have the
> principles of natural subordination by art rooted out of their
> minds. They must respect that property of which they cannot
> partake. They must labour to obtain that which by labour can
> be obtained, and when they find, as they commonly do, their

success disproportional to their endeavour, they must be
taught their consolation in the final proportions of eternal
justice... (*Reflections on the Revolution in France* Pelican,
1970, p. 372)

These deep habits of practice and thought are transmitted
and articulated so that every situation has the form and
resonates the signals of the total 'moral community'.

... In this choice of inheritance, we (the British) have given to
our frame of polity the image of a relation in blood; binding up
the constitution of our country with our deepest domesticities;
adopting our fundamental laws into the bosom of our family
affections; keeping inseparable, and cherishing with the
warmth of all their combined and mutually reflecting charities,
our states, our hearths, our sepulchres and our altars.
(*Reflections*, p.120)

More recent Marxists have come to some terms with the
power of the political 'superstructure' and have, indeed,
gone some distance towards doing away with the whole
'superstructural' mode of thinking about ideology, culture,
morality and politics. Gramsci's notion of 'hegemony'
belongs to this movement and now Althusser and his
followers stress the importance of 'the ideological
apparatuses of the state'. Nicos Poulantzas, for example,
reviewing Ralph Miliband's book *The State in Capitalist
Society* (in *New Left Review*, 58, 1969), maintains the idea
that the state is the one and only institution of political rule,
and extends the term 'state' to cover all institutions maintaining the social formation. Thus Poulantzas represents trade
unions, the mass media, the churches, the family as themselves being *state* apparatuses (curiously omitting the
capitalist firms whose 'apparatus' presumably is the state
itself). And the same things are done in Althusser's book
Lenin and Philosophy (*New Left Books*, 1971). Miliband
himself points out in reply (*New Left Review*, 59, 1970) that if
the state is analytically identified with any conservative
institution, it is difficult to see, for example, the specific
process whereby the state, in its narrow sense, fattens itself
by incorporating social institutions directly, as happens with

fascism. It is clearer to maintain the distinction between the state and its allies and agents. Poulantzas' way, which suggests that all conservative forces must have one common source in 'the state', produces a kind of analytic fascism. If, however, while resisting the broadened notion of 'the state', we do enlarge our notion of 'politics', we are able to examine the specific historically developing ways in which states work in relation to other 'political' forces in society and to understand what it means for political movements to work against, through or independently of the state.

Vulgar-marxism involves vulgar politics. And vulgar marxism has a respectable ancestry in Marx and Engels themselves. Its problem might be expressed abstractly thus: on the one hand it asserts an overwhelmingly one-way causality between base and superstructure; on the other hand, the 'base', usually amounting to technology and the wage struggle is so inadequate to support, let alone to burst the superstructure that 'political will' in the form of the state-orientated party has to be introduced as the *deus-ex-machina* that brings either stability or change into the system. A richer conception of politics and a richer conception of 'productive relations', for example, helps get politics in theory where it is in practice; at the centre of things. And this, after all, is implicit in the whole Marxian idea of class domination, class rule — a political idea if there ever was one.

Undoubtedly, the perspective being advocated here presents problems for our understanding of what politics is and in particular the problem of articulating a usefully specific notion of 'the political' to replace the conventional statist one. I have been arguing that politics should not be defined in terms of a proprietary entity, but should be thought of as a pervasive dimension of social relations - but *what* dimension of social relations? Let us look again at the standard dichotomy: political/economic. We have seen how, in the 'ordinary language' both of conservatives and radicals, 'political' is contrasted with 'economic'. Thus people speak and write of the 'relation of economic and political power', and counterpose 'economic, political, ideological and theoretical practice' or 'practico-economic and political struggle' (Engels, Lenin), so that Lenin, for example, writes in *What is to be done?*:

> ... The economic struggle of the workers against the employers for better terms in the sale of their labour-power, for better living and working conditions... Lending the economic struggle itself a political character means, therefore, striving to secure satisfaction of these trade union demands by means of administrative and legislative measures. (Moscow edition, p.61).

In these formulations, even where the suggestion is not intended, the drift is that these notions pick out different and discrete types of activity, as if you could say 'this is a political, that an economic institution' (practice, struggle, relation, etc.). But think of the ideological-political-economic activity involved in maintaining such ideological-political-economic institutions as the British royal family. Think of the religious sanctification of the state, the pompous rituals in law courts and the whole mythology of respectable business. Think of the 'economic power' of the modern state, as financier, owner, employer and shareholder, not to mention as appropriator and spender of taxes.

In the capitalist economy, those who own and thus have state-sanctioned and ideologically legitimated control over the means of production are able, more or less, to use and manage, to govern, masses of people who work for them. This control is presupposed in the extraction of profit. This state of affairs is, I suggest, best thought of as a directly political one; it is a situation in which peoples' activity is dictated, through the factory and wage structures, by more or less remote bosses. It is also a situation, of course, where workers, in more or less organised and more or less official ways (the two ways are not synonymous), influence the conditions under which they work. A brief reading of any management or 'industrial relations' journal will reveal that, to the bosses, the political character of the situation is not lost.

Struggles in the factory, then, are political struggles according to this way of seeing things, and the poverty of 'economism' is not an absence of politics but a poverty of politics. To say that a production situation is political is not to say that it is only political. It seems to me most satisfactory to think of social relations of production as political *and* economic relations, apart from any other characters they may have, and to think of these concepts as referring to different aspects of the 'total' situation. Thus, to speak of 'the economy' is to abstract, is not to be dealing with a discrete 'part' of society. It is not as though the economic 'relations of production' give rise to something else, namely 'political' relations. Rather, these productive relations are political relations, and in capitalist society they are relations of qualified and contested domination by capitalists over workers.

From an 'economic' standpoint, the focus is on resources and the action of labour on them to produce something. From this stand-point, the worker, *qua* producer, is a more or less productive unit. Under this aspect, his rebelliousness or docility are economic variables as much as skill or strength are. Power and authority relations are subsumed under the terms of 'economic organisation' or 'the technical division of labour'. The 'politics' of the situation involves a different focus, interdependent with the economic. The situation from this standpoint is one of domination and of more or less open struggle. Even a simple exchange situation, after all, involves parties having control of some good 'over and against' the other. From a political standpoint the economic need of the worker to produce his means of existence gives the controllers of the means of production control over him. Thus, just as 'force is itself an economic power' (Marx) so wealth is itself a political power, an instrument of control.

Emphasising 'aspects' over 'entities' clarifies the notions of 'the forces and relations of production'. Often, with thoughts of Marx's hand-mill and steam-mill in mind, some Marxists tend to focus on the mechanical embodiments of technology as 'productive forces', while the way people combine to act on and with these instruments is called 'productive relations'. Now part of the trouble with this approach, and one which is a mark of Soviet-inspired development theory, is that the human relations of production tend to be relegated to mere means to the maximisation of 'productive forces'. What gets ignored here is the fact that the organisation, skill and co-operative disposition of humans in their relations of work are themselves crucial determinants of productive potential, so that one has the situation where it has to be said that human productive relations *are* productive forces. Thus, if the 'forces and relations' locution is retained, its meaning might best be seen as identical with the 'economic/political' distinction as drawn here. One advantage of this is that it directly highlights the 'politics' of technology, emphasising questions of freedom and control and subverting the usual drift of technocratic ways of thought, which conceal political questions behind pseudo-impartial claims of efficiency, or of 'the imperatives of development'.

That viewpoint, which takes 'the economy' as a solidary whole whose health is measured by such indices as 'gross national product', regularly leaves out of account the 'economic standpoint' of the workers themselves - the costs and benefits to them of the way their lives are organised - and regularly omits from the balance sheet the disutilities of pollution and the impoverishment of people's living environments, the rubble left by capitalism's progress. I have contrasted 'the political' with 'the economic', but this is not to *deny* that much talk of 'the economy, with its false suggestion of a monolithic social enterprise, belongs primarily to the political art of capitalists and statesmen. Roughly, then, I am suggesting that, while 'political' questions are questions of the balance of power, 'economic' questions are questions of the balance of welfare.

If, as it is urged more concretely in the next chapter, we see industrial relations as political relations, we loosen ourselves from the Official Labour Party dichotomy of 'industrial' (trade union) and 'political' (party) spheres; these cumbersome wings of the 'Labour Movement', a dichotomy which reduces working-class political activity to defensive bargaining and petty amelioration inside the framework of capitalist rule and actively blinkers workers from contesting capitalist despotism and state authoritarianism in the factory or at a wider level. Like priests caught in a brothel, trade union leaders still ritually feel obliged to deny that their activities are political, even when, 'in the interests of our members' they bring pressure to bear on governments. The British government-union 'social contract' has subverted this dichotomy from the right; bringing T.U.C. officials into a semi-governmental status as managers of working-class discontent, so that Mr. Len Murray appears as a 'politician' in almost the way that Mr. James Callaghan does. The danger for the trade-union bureaucrat thus enmeshed of course is that by losing even the posture of opposition the official leaves room open for the development of a different, unofficial type of opposition, hence for a different type of industrial politics in which the political question of control is more sharply posed. From this perspective strikes are political acts, whose frequent defect is bad politics not the absence of politics. More generally, political conflict over production takes many different, official and unofficial, forms on both sides. Certainly the ruling class does not restrict its warfare to the official type. It may work, 'legitimately' or 'illegitimately' through the state, an instrument finely adapted to that function. But it may not. It works constantly through the media presenting its public servant image of 'Industry'. It works through industrial relations departments. 'Direct action' is not foreign to it: from boycotts to finance strikes it has its unofficial means of maintaining its position, of remaining in charge of the masses it needs to exploit. And more mundanely, as will be discussed later, it works through the workaday harness of the wage and factory system themselves.

Levels of Politics

The idea that politics, far from being the proper sphere of a particular institution, is best seen as a fundamental dimension of human life implicitly opens up another break from the usual statist picture. For if it is accepted that workers in a factory stand in a political relation to their bosses, we also have to see politics at different and interpenetrating levels, low and high, micro and macro. We have, that is, to get away from seeing politics solely on a national scale, and take seriously the idea, not only of 'local politics', but of the politics of particular families, groups, schools, hospitals, prisons. It is not for nothing that the state has been seen on the model of the family, the family on the model of a factory ('for the production of authoritarian ideology' - Wilhelm Reich, *The Sexual Revolution*), the factory on the model of a prison, the prison on the model of a school... and *vice versa* all down the line. What is being brought out by these parallels is the common structure and the mutual reinforcement of the dominant institutions of our society.

Statism, the identification of politics with the state, developed and flourished as an ideology of the would-be sovereign nation-state. But, while states are a major political force and, given their existence and power, shape any political movement that comes into being, they are not the only political force, or even necessarily the dominant political force in social life. World politics cannot be tacked on to political theory as if states related to each other and to international forces like bourgeois neighbours in suburbia. The atomistic idea of independent sovereign states was always an illusion; but the very project of the European Common Market shows its contemporary inadequacy even at the official level. Huge corporations, sometimes 'foreign' or 'multinational', have the power to rock or even sink the ship of state, and to transform the lives of people supposedly protected thereby. Yet British political philosophers, oblivious to the neo-colonialism of their kith and kin in business and foreign office, and amnesic about Empire, write as if the maintenance within national boundaries (and within reason) of forms and rituals amounted to the maintenance of national political self-government, as if decency in one country were a realistic vision.

If the state's pretensions as the agent of harmony are questionable, the harmony of the state itself needs examining. Certainly a monolithic view of the state is natural in Britain (read 'England'), where the public school and Oxbridge channels have produced a uniquely cohesive ruling stratum, preponderant in party, civil service, military and judiciary - as well as in all spheres of official 'political thought'. But as events in such places as Chile have brought home, different state institutions and tendencies, including

class tendencies, within these institutions can be in bloody
political conflict. And even 'at home', bureaucratic
departments, parliamentarians, law-lords, are constantly at
odds with one another, clogged internally and externally,
unable to achieve even their official objectives. The official
view ignores the informal politics that positions within the
state institutions facilitate; patronage, graft, turning a blind
eye - all sorts of uncivilised conduct, the control of which is
the state's official mission' - flourish within its permissive
walls. So, if we go below and above the official level, we see
that state politics, when looked at in terms of real power-
relations and real processes, need not be at all the
principle-bound affair it is presented as.

Below the national level, there are political forms and
tensions in religions, towns, neighbourhoods, families, not to
mention schools and colleges. Now of course, these
institutions are a more or less integral part of a wider political
structure, part of 'the system'; they canot be understood in
isolation. If socialism in one country is an illusory hope,
socialism in one factory - or family! - is a dream. But to say
this is not to accept that conflict at these levels cannot have
considerable independence from wider alignments; there are
international leftist academics who are pillars of academic
authority in their own place of work, militant workers who
vote for conservative parties, and revolutionaries-at-large
whose house is a feudal manor. These are best seen as
contradictions within people's politics, not as conflicts
between their politics and something else — 'their personal
lives'.

To say that the school or family is a political institution
is, so far, not to say anything very determinate. 'The school'
(or 'schools-in-general'), is nowadays clearly a state
institution, as well as being part of the institutional structure
of the 'political system' in the widest sense. Moreover, what
goes on in particular schools can be 'political' in a fairly
conventional sense: for example, conflicts over state
requirements over comprehensivisation or desegregation.
What goes on in a particular classroom will be 'political' in
the sense of being influenced by the needs and demands of
the ruling national or international order. But it is not only an

individual school or classroom's political causes or effects that constitutes its 'politics': what goes on in *this* classroom, with teacher Mr. Jones or Miss Smith, according to the perspective being advocated, is political 'in itself'. And so it is with a particular family or factory.

All the classical questions of 'political philosophy' apply to schools, factories, families, to any human relations: questions of 'obedience', of 'legitimate authority', of 'consent', of 'freedom', of 'justice', of 'democracy', of 'equality', of 'the common interest', and so on. Production, of food for example, can be more or less free, more or less just, more or less democratic. It is not a good sign that the state alone fills the category of 'The Political' when 'the sorts of things it makes sense to say and ask about it' can be said and asked about so many other things and their interrelationships. To those who deny this and claim that the special features of the territorial nation-state constitute it as a philosophically special entity, the question would be: what is the difference?

By calling a structure or situation 'political', we are stressing the tension and at least potential conflict among the activities and interests that make it up. That these structures persist is a function of the continued co-operation among the different forces within them, co-operation sometimes given literally on pain of death. The carrying on of human activities requires the continuing support, co-operation, acquiescence or submission of other activities, or at an extreme, their destruction. Activities, then, can interrelate in a more or less free, more or less just, more or less democratic way: these are the key parameters of social life, and political activity is activity maintaining, contesting, or transforming, more or less deeply, more or less superficially, such 'forms'. How activities interrelate will obviously depend on what sort of activities they are. Some, such as the drudgery of factory labour, of their very nature presuppose dominance — submission relations and require the elaborate backing of state apparatuses: a politics of 'nationalisation' in these circumstances would obviously be, by itself, a superficial politics, leaving people's way of life in many ways funda-mentally unchanged. 'The working class cannot simply lay hold of the ready made state machinery and wield it for its own purposes.'

Philosophical statism freezes the imagination within the official compartments. Alternative visions, whether in the minds of radical thinkers or in the practice of revolutionary movements, are excluded from the academic argument. *The Anarchist Reader,* Ed. George Woodcock (Harvester and Fontana) is a valuable antidote). To get beyond statist apologetics, even to get far enough to turn back to see what could be learned from it, would require unearthing these visions, and, in particular, rediscovering the movements - especially the communes and the workers councils, that have sought to replace state and capitalist rule with radical democracy.

CHAPTER 2

THE POLITICS OF PRODUCTION

Labour: Philosophy's Suppressed Premiss

In *Useful Work Versus Useless Toil*, William Morris advised his contemporaries not to take received pieties about the economic and moral value of 'civilised' work for granted, but 'to look into the matter a little deeper'. The advice is still needed. Certainly contemporary academic philosophers, in Britain at least, shy off the subject. When they write, for example, about justice or equality, they write about the principles according to which people should be 'treated', and that usually means principles according to which their money-income and hence their consumption should be determined and 'services', such as 'health', provided, usually by that earthly Providence, the state; thus the concern is with 'distributive' justice. When they talk about freedom they counterpose it to welfare, again thought of as a consumption-centred variable ('goods'!), and discuss the 'proper balance' of freedom and welfare. In general, then, the frame of reference is the problems of the welfare-state and little attention is focused on the inequality and unfreedom of this whole-state-managerial framework. That most adults in our society spend most of their waking lives working to earn a living, or working domestically to make it possible for others to earn a living, that children spend their days at school preparing for such a life, gets ignored. That most people's work is a tedious and stultifying grind, that there is injustice, unfreedom, inequality, authoritarian government, pain and misery in production gets ignored. If our philosophers of law and punishment show little signs of having been near a gaol, let alone in one, the walls of our factories are equally remote from the thought and experience of our philosophers of justice, freedom, 'human action' ('I raise my arm all day') and bodily sensation ('Question 6: Distinguish tiredness from fatigue'). To those whose freedom to pursue inquiry for its own sake as a profession rests on the fact that others lack it, the drudgery of the masses working lives appears to be, if not a natural, than a technical phenomenon, beyond argument. We live 'when all is said and done' in an 'advanced industrial society', and as school examinations and I.Q. tests show, only a minority are capable of mastering its complexities - the simple majority can expect no more than to be subject to them. And are there not powerful trade unions,who 'can usually insist that workers interests be considered'? (Benn and Peters, *Social Principles and the Democratic* State, p.165) The two most notable works of academic political philosophy in recent years: *A Theory of Justice* by John Rawls and *Anarchy, State and Utopia* by Robert Nozick, illustrate in different ways the structural blindness I am talking about.

The Social Contract and the Labour Contract: John Rawls

Working life as we have seen in Chapter 1, occupies a peripheral place in John Rawls' *Theory of Justice*. Asserting 'the priority of liberty', he locates the basic liberties wholly within the sphere of the accepted bourgeois civil liberties and fails to see that tyrannical disenfranchisement is the normal lot of the worker, both within capitalist industry as we now have it and within the 'well ordered society' that his theory envisages. Rawls simply assumes that production will be hierarchically organised and that positions in the hierarchy will have very disparate financial and status rewards attached to them. All will be just, as long as these differences are to the advantage of the 'worst off' by increasing production and increasing the income of those at the bottom, whether directly through wages, or 'from outside' through progressive taxation or welfare payments. As to whether industry should be organised capitalistically or socialistically, Rawls says his theory is 'neutral' (p. 274). And the secondary importance of 'economic' institutions is further emphasised by Rawls' claim that injustices involving the 'difference principle', that inequalities must benefit the worst off, unlike injustices involving the 'principle of equal liberty', are not proper grounds for civil disobedience. (Let them continue eating cake, as long as they have the vote.)

The heart of Rawls' dualism in an unstated assumption that, 'the economy' is essentially a mere instrument to consumption goals, a site where valued things are made, and incomes with which to buy those valued things are earned. The politics, ethics, and aesthetics of productive life itself are thus ignored, and Rawls is able to come up with the absurd idea that equality in the social bases of self-respect is guaranteed without reference to productive organisation. This, together with the elitist assumption, pervading Rawls' book, of crucial innate differences in 'talent' and 'motivation', hinders him from bringing productive life into steady focus and from applying to that the liberal-democratic canons he brings to bear on other areas of social life. In that case, even within Rawls' own terms, the illiberal and undemocratic nature of capitalist, not to mention 'state-socialist', productive forms would have been revealed.

Rawls' blindness on this issue is made striking by the fact that, when he comes to fill out his conception of a good society, when he complements the 'thin' theory (in whose terms the basic framework just criticised was established) with a 'full' theory, Rawls emphasises values of community, mutuality, and creativity, in ways that the basic framework makes no allowance for. Thus he asserts the 'Aristotelian Principle' according to which:

> 'other things being equal, human beings enjoy the exercise of their realised capacities (their innate or trained abilities), and this enjoyment increases the more the capacity is realised, or greater its complexity' (p. 426)

But not only does Rawls fail to examine the conditions under which this value could be realised, he simply assumes elsewhere that the very minority who can enjoy stretching their capacities, the entrepreneurs, will need great wealth and prestige to motivate their activity. Thus the 'Aristotelian Principle', despite its allegedly central place in Rawls' account of human good, plays no clear role in the basic structure of his theory.

So it is for other values which Rawls avows: On p. 440 and following, he discusses the conditions of self-respect in a spirit out of keeping with his earlier emphasis on 'equality of citizenship'. Self-respect, linked with the Aristotelian principle, is seen to be a function of 'public affirmation' of the character and worth of people's life-activities. Now Rawls does not see this idea as *prima facie* radical in its implication, he does not see it as condemning the humiliating and useless ways in which masses of people are employed. His way out is the separate 'legalitarianism' of a sort of apartheid:

> 'In a well ordered society there are a variety of communities and associations, and the members of each have their own ideals appropriately matched to their own ideals and aspirations' (p. 441)

Hacks and minions of the world unite; you have nothing to lose but your membership fees!

Rawls's attempt to carve a human face on the cold granite of western social institutions fails because the aspirations for justice that infuse the book are vitiated by Rawls' engulfment in the conventional structures of bourgeois society. Any attempt to develop an adequate conception of social justice would have to take Rawls's analysis into account, but it would have to begin with a wider and more radical vision than he found possible. (Gerald Doppelt's (unpublished) critique develops this theme in depth.)

The Piglet Philosophy: R.A. Nozick

R.A. Nozick has some things to say about work in his widely praised book *Anarchy, State and Utopia* (Blackwells, 1974, especially Chapter 8). The book is a defence of the rights of owners against state interference, its message is that you are entitled to have what you own. Nozick calls himself a 'libertarian' and makes great rhetorical play of the bullying interventionism of the allegedly 'redistributionist' or 'welfare' state. But when it comes to the protection of property Nozick is a member of the law-and-order brigade, and when it comes to control of working people's working lives he belongs to the orthodox regimental school. In short, Nozick is a 'free-enterprise' man.

Nozick has a short way with all this 'Rawlsian' talk about equality of self-respect. Self-respect, says Nozick, is essentially invidious. Considering Trotsky's olympian vision of a time when 'the average human type will rise to the heights of an Aristotle, a Goethe, or a Marx. And above this ridge new peaks will rise', Nozick remarks that the unfortunate average human will then feel pretty inadequate as, from the level of a mere Marx, he looks up at the new peaks. The comment on Trotsky's formulation the comment is apt. But Nozick insists on a general moral:

> People generally judge themselves by how they fall along the most important dimensions in which they differ from others. People do not gain self-esteem from their common human capacities... Self esteem is based on differentiating characteristics: that's why it's *self*-esteem... (p. 243)

As an expression of the fate of the ego in an individualistic and competitive culture such as that of capitalist societies, Nozick's remarks are pertinent. Within such societies, rooted as they are in maintaining scarcity as a condition of maintaining value-price-and-profit, invidious 'differentiation' of product and of personality, occupies a central place. Hence it matters, not so much whether you have a good thing or do a good job, as whether you have what others lack or do what others haven't done, a veritable recipe for manic-depressive psychosis. But it is possible and common even in our culture for people to take pride in the adequate performance of valued tasks, where the pride comes principally from 'the object' and the activity, only secondarily from the receipt of special praise. A boat builder is happy if his boat has what a boat needs; he doesn't need a reserve army of incompetents to maintain his self-esteem. Using competitive games as his paradigm, Nozick says that 'there is no standard of doing something well independent of how it is done or can be done by others' (p. 241). But this is utterly distorted - a boat either floats or it doesn't, a fishing net either holds or it doesn't, people either can do mouth-to-mouth resuscitation or they cannot, and such things are valued without the need for point-scoring and all the paraphernalia of winning and losing with which Nozick is so preoccupied. Nozick's idea that there have to be losers blinds him to the culturally specific viciousness of a system that confines human beings to jobs which, however the fact might be disguised by wage-differentials and competitions for the tidiest kitchen, are tedious, degrading, and, as often as not, useless.

Nozick then considers the idea that 'meaningful work' is a condition of self-esteem and that the mechanical repetitiveness and subordination characteristic of capitalist industry should be done away with. But, says Nozick, look at the ordinary members of symphony orchestras, army draftees, socialist factory organisers, 'persons on the way up organisational ladders'. Such people do not suffer lack of self-esteem (p. 246). Well, that is questionable. But suppose Nozick is right - let us ask why. People who get into symphony orchestras enjoy contributing to something beautiful. They also enjoy a certain prestige. Draftees, assuming a random draft process, cannot think that their subordination is a function of their own failings (unless in respect of their failure to dodge the draft). Socialist factory organisers exercise initiative during working hours challenging the power of a class whose position they consider illegitimate. They do not see their own or their workmates subordination as a function of personal shortcomings; that's part of their socialism. Nozick's idealised young men on their way to the top, given that they are truly upward-bound, perceive their present subordination as a temporary necessity, as part of their career: they will not be demoralised or attribute their position to personal failings. In all cases we do not have that characteristic situation of the subject classes in liberal capitalist society where myths of equality of opportunity and social mobility meet realities of static hierarchies and mindless life-long drudgery to induce that sense of personal failure, of damaged and low self-esteem, that is so characteristic of working-class psychology. The question of self-respect, self-esteem, and of the psychology of class is much more complex than this brief rebuttal suggests. But there is little evidence that Nozick has thought about it very much at all.

Nozick hints that the reason for workers low self-esteem may be that they *are* personally inferior and know it (pp. 246-7) and that subordinates', defeatist psychology:

THE POLITICS OF PRODUCTION 51

... may be due to the fact that those predisposed to show low independent activity are just those who are most willing to take and remain with certain jobs involving little opportunity for independent flowering. (p. 248)

Think of the assembly-line and the domestic workplace of women as a kind of asylum for the unenterprising! Looking at our schools and bearing in mind that career 'success' is generally a function of number of years spent in them, we might well conclude that the opportunity to do independent things in later life is a reward for refraining from them in earlier life. But if Nozick is ignorant of the processes preparing people for 'their place', he is ignorant too of the bitter struggle that capitalist industrialists had to wage to bring production under their control and out of the relatively free hands of the artisan class. The drudgery-habituated worker inhabits the site of centuries' battles and defeats.

Nozick assumes (pp. 248,251) that since capitalists and unions have not invested in firms which provide meaningfu work or are under workers' control, such forms of production must be less efficient. Nor are such forms of production attractive to workers, who are fortunate enough to be able to 'choose among their employment activities on the basis of the overall package of benefits it gives them' (p. 249). But, as the U.S. government's special commission concluded in its study *Work in America* (M.I.T. Press, 1973), the introduction of more 'meaningful' and autonomous job patterns in certain firms has proved profitable. Moreover, you cannot equate capitalist profitability with capacity for efficiency in production. Given a situation where a boss wants to get as much out of his workers as possible and given the contrary disposition on the part of the workforce, it is in the boss's interest to establish as much control over the work process and product as he can - otherwise his subordinates will exercise their initiative in avoiding work or appropriating for themselves some of the product. The reduction of work to maximally controllable and accountable units, in other words, is in large measure a function of the fundamental opposition in the production situation itself. And this reflects itself in the fact that the schemes of 'meaningful work' that have been tried and have succeeded are in factories where there is little

history of militancy or insubordination. A problem for
Nozick: in capitalist-initiated amelioration of work, inviting
the subordinates to exercise initiative, is successful precisely
among workers who on other grounds could be said to be
unenterprising and obedient.

Nozick wonders (p. 250) why workers have not gone in for
worker-controlled firms, setting up 'micro-industrial
schemes' within the capitalist economy. Such questions, like
questions of the continuing subjection of women, require
historical exploration and it is a sort of insult to consider them
within the framework of *a priori* psychology. Nozick talks
about workers leaving 'risk' to big investors. But a big
investor, unlike a proletarian co-operative, is able to mini-
mise by diversifying; the risk to him of a factory's failure,
unlike his employees his eggs are in many baskets. Given the
pressures and vagaries of a system of production for profit, it
is little wonder that most 'worker-control' orientated proletarians look to smash the capitalist system rather than to set
up vulnerable islands of co-operativism within that system.

Nozick attacks the general idea that 'people have a right to
a say in the decisions that importantly affect their own lives'
(p. 269). He brings up two putative 'counter-examples':
Toscanini's leaving an orchestra, he says, 'importantly
affects' its members; but that doesn't give them the right to a
say in Toscanini's decision. Now, talk of rights here may be
obscuring, for there is no question that Toscanini *ought* to
give weight to the impact of his leaving on an orchestra -
whether that amounts to their having a right to *a say,* which is
not a right to decide, is unclear to me. But note the
pecularities of the case: it's Toscanini, so the orchestra has
been extremely lucky to work with him. He hasn't entered a
situation where the established expectation is that he is a
member of a sovereign, mutually beneficial collective. But if
we want to ask the general question whether orchestras
should be so organised, whether such rights should be
defended, Nozick's example leaves us dangling; for its force
depends on the very features of the *status quo,* the established expectations, that it seeks to support. So it is with Nozick's
second example, that of lending someone a bus for a year and
finding on your return that it has become important to the

borrowers' lives so that it might be claimed that they therefore have a right to a say in who keeps it. Again the talk of rights is obscuring, for it suggests clear criteria of whether or not a right exists. In England, for example, squatters 'have' rights similar to those whose existence Nozick is denying. But, given that private property in motor cars persists with all its attendant expectations, needs, and obligations, Nozick's claim to have his bus back has a *prima facie* force. Notice that he (generously) lent it, that it, like Toscanini, is a big unreciprocated bonus to its beneficiaries. Notice too, as the examples get mentioned in the broad context of an attack on industrial democrats, that neither example is a case of people not having a right to a say in the government of their own lives, to a say, for example, over whether they are fired from a job. To establish the general injustice of such a demand, Nozick would have to be prepared to defend by parity of reasoning the idea that as long as positions of governmental authority were bought and sold on the open market, those subject to such authority should not think their rights were being violated. Even Nozick might shrink from that position. Certainly the capitalist boss stands in a different relation to his employees from that in which Toscanini stands to his orchestra or a lender to a borrower. Nozick abstracts details of every day life under capitalism and uses them to defend the structure within which those examples have their very intelligibility. Any social system can be defended by that method.

That Nozick should consider it philosophically relevant to attack the workers' control movement signifies a major advance in thought, for it marks the end of a period when the conditions under which people spend much of their waking lives, like other subjects not fit for polite conversation, have exercised a latent but unacknowledged impact on the whole framework of philosophicl inquiry, from moral philosophy to aesthetics. Nozick, though clearly ignorant of the things about which he writes, at least has the hide to write about them. And once people start to look at the way work is organised in our society, it will emerge that publicity for capitalist industry is bad publicity.

Rawls and Nozick, then, do at least help us to force

questions about working life into critical focus. But there has always been a kind of unconscious recognition in philosophy of the centrality of labour to life. Think, for example, of 'utilitarianism'. Officially, the utilitarians' concern was with maximising happiness. What was their conception of happiness?: the preponderance of pleasure over pain. What was their conception of pleasure?: as a sensation albeit a bloodless one, for the sake of which people, otherwise inert, will act. 'Happiness', then, became reduced to a balance of atomic pleasures, and pleasures were conceived of as sensations while, in Bentham's workhouse-philosophy, drudgery, 'rewarded' by the absence of starvation, constitutes the reasonable expectation of the mass of mankind. Life, as a more or less coherent, joyful, and harmonious pattern of activities, involvements and experiences, seems to be passed by, and the idea of a happy life, as a, if not *the,* central ideal of existence is twisted into Bentham's calculus of sensations. What has been the academic fate of utilitarianism? On the one hand moral philosophers still embrace or reject it within its own terms, within its own inadequate notion of happiness. On the other hand, philosophers, especially since Gilbert Ryle reported from his pleasure-garden, have shown up the shortcomings in the Benthamite notion of pleasure, but have been content to focus on atomic activities, pleasurable pastimes on the whole, just as Bentham focused on atomic sensations. With the exception of Dewey *(The Theory of the Moral Life),* no major Anglo-American academic philosopher has, as far as I know, sought to replace the Benthamite notion of happiness with one which is both activity-centred and respects the fact that human life cannot be assessed in atoms but needs to be looked at holistically. And, as far as I know, Dewey is the only major mainstream philosopher to recognise the centrality of production, not only as a means to consumption, but as the key ingredient of our 'moral environment'. He wrote, for example, 'until the mass of men and women who do the useful work of the world have the opportunity to be free in conducting the process of production and are richly endowed in the capacity for enjoying the fruits of collective work', society's moral, aesthetic, political, and psychological culture will be divided and impoverished

(Art as Experience, Capricorn, 1958, p. 344). Dewey, then, was concerned with the conditions of a happy society, and to a considerable extent faced up to the radical implications of that concern. Our more conventional contemporaries, on the contrary, restrict their focus to consumer and leisure pleasures, acquiescing by default in the very splits that Dewey was concerned to attack. It remains the case that the stupefied tedium of *Brave New World* is the dominant image of a society where the greatest happiness is enjoyed by the greatest number, and that the sensuous, the experiential, and the social character of pleasure has been denied by people who reduce pleasure to the attainment of 'preferences'. This, then, is one respect in which the philosophers and economists combine to consecrate the poverty of everyday life, while the overall dualism and authoritarianism of the academic view of the world conforms to what might be expected from the mandarins of a split society.

Not unusually, however, our philosophers are behind even *The Times,* for the politics of work is now out in the open; indeed the question of 'industrial democracy' is already acquiring the label 'fashionable' (see, for example, Alasdair Clayre's article 'Merits of Workers' Control in Industry' in *The Times,* as far back as 19 September 1969). As is noted in the report of a conference among 'managerial experts' of the International Organisation for Economic Co-operation and Development (O.E.C.D.):

> Whereas twenty years ago there was little or no call from the trade union movement for workers' control, for the assumption of managerial authority by the workers themselves, this call is now very strong in some Western countries. These trends show that the basic authority of management, namely its right to manage at all, is now increasingly challenged. ('The Emerging Attitudes and Motivations of Workers', report by R.W. Revans, February 1972, unpublished)

Free Slavery: Wage-Labour in Capitalist Society

A man or woman sells the use of his working capacity to the owners of a firm and receives a wage or a salary.

'Ordinary language' acknowledges the worker's debt by functionally defining the organisation he signs up for as 'the employer', which 'provides' him with employment; the organisation is then further functionally defined as 'the management' and further as a member of that great collectivity 'Industry': again, 'ordinary language' puts everything in order - by definition. The employee goes to work; in a factory, say. There he has to fit into a structure of machine and human capital geared as it is to maximum productivity consistent with stability of profit for its owners. To this end, and to keep his job in its service, he has to submit to managers, supervisors, and foremen, work certain definite hours, stay on the job except at certain 'break' times; in general to obey the dictates of the production-process, its agents and its controllers:

> You just about need a pass to piss. That ain't no joke. You raise your hand if you want to go wee-wee. Then wait maybe half an hour till they find a relief man. And they write it down every time too - because you're supposed to do it in your own time, not theirs. Try it too often and you'll get a week off. (General Motors assembly-line worker, quoted in *The Lordstown Struggle,* Solidarity Pamphlet, London, 1974)

Certainly the worker 'freely contracted' to enter this situation; he can leave if he wants to; he can even take steps of self-improvement to put himself in a situation to boss others around (there have to be some such others). Such is the capitalist picture of free labour, a picture which, in its eulogy of the wage-worker's liberty, forgets that even the slave can choose to risk the lash. Against Sir Isaiah Berlin's view of freedom as choice *(Two Concepts of Liberty),* it is necessary to insist that freedom depends on the worth and importance of the options and on the socially conditioned capacity of an individual to assess those options; freedom is not just a matter of the *number* of things a person is allowed to do. (For a discussion of this, see Benjamin Gibbs' *Freedom and Liberation,* S.U.P. 1976.) And in conditions where the means to produce, even at a subsistence level, are out of his hands or control, the male without independent means or background must, given his 'resources and qualifications', make a choice from amoung the available factories, try to survive on the dole, or chance living outside the law. His female counterpart has the additional option of looking after a home and family. The labour-market, as Bentham understood well enough, functions to a large extent coercively; it is a mechanism by which, on pain of something worse, the worker has to subject himself to the despotism of his individual or corporate boss.

Unionism as Democracy

Freedom-as-contract maintains a more or less healthy existence as a justifying ideology of 'the free world's' industrial life. Nowadays, however, the existence of trade-unions is widely held to be the guarantee, as long as modest and reasonable limits are observed, of proletarian freedom, of industrial democracy, and of distributive justice in the wage-packet. Through their capacity for collective withholding of labour, it is thought, unions, by definition, cancel out capitalist dominance over the workers taken individually. We have a 'balance'; indeed current Tory thinking in Britain seems to be that the balance has swung so far in favour of the unions that industrial militants now constitute the ruling class. But in general the idea is that we do have a balance. The Trade Union Council seems to have thought so; and its favoured post-war theorist, Hugh Clegg, has summed up the neo-liberal philosophy of industrial citizenship thus:

> ... in all the stable democracies there is a system of industrial relations which can fairly be called the industrial parallel of political democracy. (*A New Approach to Industrial Democracy*, Blackwells, 1960, p. 131)

Is Clegg right? It is questionable to what extent our societies are either stable or democratic in any case; our oligarchies-under-electoral-influence are desperately trying to manage the chaos they contribute to. More directly, it is questionable to what extent trade unions, with the corrupting quasi-managerial sinecures they provide for the career - 'representatives' of working people, can be entitled the spokesmen and guardians of the shop floor. As a sectional-

ised and constitutionalised opposition to certain aspects of
corporate prerogatives, the trade union position in the class
structure is inherently ambiguous, and this ambiguity is
reflected in the frequency with which workers act unofficially
and against their 'leaders' advice. But all these points apply
to 'representatives' in the national governments of 'liberal
democracies'; they don't subvert Clegg's analogy. Are trade-
unions analogous to a parliamentary opposition? Hardly; for
the parallel would require the constitutional possibility of
workers electing, not merely a permanent opposition, but an
industrial government. But, as is still required by company
law, and insisted on by the Confederation of British Industry,
'management' is responsible, not to the workforce subject to
it, but to the owners or shareholders. A better analogy,
therefore, would be the sort of limited authority that a
colonial power might grant to a native assembly which
'represents' the indigenes but is subject to the colonial
administrators, themselves responsible to the imperial government. Workers are capitalism's restless natives. To insist
thus on the subject-status of workers is not to deny that they,
or their unions, have great power. But, leaving aside the
potentiality within the working class to rise up and overthrow
the capitalist regime, it is important to distinguish different
powers here. That underlings have the power to disrupt a
system and thus to force concessions within it does not alter
their underling status. That a system which depends on a
low-wage economy, like Britain's, can be thrown out of
balance by movement for less low wages does not imply that
there exists a 'balance' between capital and labour that has
anything to do with justice or equality. That the dominated
have some power does not mean that they are not dominated.

In general, as is implicitly recognised in the Labour
Research Department's *Industrial Democracy: a Trade-
Unionist's Guide,* (London, 1976) the oppositionist politics
of trade unionism is within the despotic framework of our
industrial system. The very multiplicity of unions follows the
divisions in the labour force effected by and functional to
capitalism. The very fact that unions' main activity is to
'bargain' over the price of labour means, in the context of an
unstable and competitive market, that they have to be careful

not to price their members out of a job, either by 'excessive' wage-demands or by 'excessive' demands for decent job-conditions, security, or safety. Capitalism needs its workers 'on the cheap' and, since workers need a job, they have to cheapen themselves if they want to be acceptable. In any case, the 'free' market enables labour costs to be passed on as commodity prices to 'The Consumer', this passive, isolated, helpless, and pitiful creature being none other than the worker and his or her family *qua* domestic unit. And so, even in 'good periods', when workers' initiatives and struggles are able to make often marginal and temporary gains, the worker is still trapped in the factory barracks. Bert Ramelson of the British Communist Party says that the right to strike is 'the be-all and end-all of the industrial trade union struggle' (*Marxism Today,* October 1968). Certainly the capacity to strike is a necessary condition of industrial freedom, but such a merely negative capacity is far from being a sufficient condition of that freedom.

Freedom-as-trade-unionism expresses the hierarchical outlook of contemporary bureaucrats. It is taken as given that the worker is in the position of subject and that management is the function of (what else?) 'Management'. As John Davies, in his capacity as Director-General of the Confederation of British Industry truistically proclaimed: 'The people responsible for enterprises are the decision-makers' *(The Times,* July 1968). It is taken as given, then, that the function of workers is to get on with (what else?) work. Indeed, in their report of 1971, *Workers' Particip-ation in Management*, Roberts, Clarke and Fatchett of the London School of Economics followed standard practice in defining 'worker' as one '... who works under contract of employment but does not have appreciable executive autho-rity' (p. 4). Then they go on to ask about the extent to which 'management' should 'involve' workers in management. To accept the framework within which these questions are usually raised as one of freedom, justice or democracy requires seeing the worker as, like a worker bee, by nature a 'worker', the fulfilment of whose capacities consists in bar-gaining for a modicum of renumeration for his humble ('though none the less real for all that') contribution. Yet it is

precisely this sort of feudal functionalism that pulses out from
the ordinary-language orchestras of the B.B.C. and the
newspapers, with their constant bckground-music about 'us
all' having contributions and sacrifices to make, as if a
shortened yachting trip could be equated with the inability to
make even the most modest ends meet.

Today, however, and despite the disciplining threat of
even more unemployment, consensus industrial politics and
the cosy conceptual network that shores it up have eroded
along with the classical capitalist work-ethic. Wildcat strikes,
riots, occupations, absenteeism, and indiscipline broke out in
a world plague in the late 1960s. The old workhouse morality
seemed to have eroded. The loyal opposition of the trade
unions was unable for a time to function as a framework for
shop-floor demands, while, especially among young people,
white and black, new to the proletarian way of life and
softened by the consumerism of the post-depression-and-war
-years, the slavery of menial work was widely rejected out of
hand. (A police inspector in London was recently complain-
ing to me about the number of young people who were not
'genuinely unemployed' and who were afraid of 'an honest
day's work'.) Thus even at a time of relative 'buoyancy'
industrial reserves were hard to tap and rapid turnover was
making training costs prohibitive for businesses. Huge com-
plexes found themselves, despite and because of their world-
wide hunt for a cheap and docile workforce, clumsily vulnerable to strikes and to unpredictable shortages of manpower
and components, so that, in the absence of total harmony,
their radical instability became evident. Thus forced to
philosophise, the more aware industrial rulers pondered The
Foundations of their Authority. At the same time as companies were resorting to the short-term expedients of speed-
ups and sackings, managerial liberals, including, in 1977,
H.M. Government's Bullock Committee, re-emerged with
schemes whereby workers could 'participate' in the decisions
that govern their lives. And so, as attempts are made to
constitute a new kind of working ethic, the battle for
discipline and productivity is fought with two faces.

At least two faces. For schemes of 'participation' range
from so-called co-ownership, whereby, as in the John Lewis

Partnership in Britain, workers enjoy the possession of a few (non-voting) shares in the company's fortunes, to deter-mination' or directorships, whereby trade union officials get to participate in 'policy' decisions at board-level, while leaving the 'details' of management to the usual well-briefed professional bureautechs. Not surprisingly, many British workers incline to be contemptuous of these schemes. Trade union bureaucrats are more and more tempted by the boardroom, but they realise, as the debates at the Trade Union Council Congress in 1974 and 1975 showed, that, if capitalism is to continue, its chief beneficiaries' decisions have to be governed by the 'law of the market'. Hence 'unpopular decisions' are inevitable and hence full-blown collusion in such decisions might threaten to loosen still further the union officials' already tenuous hold over the working people themselves. As they are not doing badly in the capitalist industrial hierarchy it is not surprising that union officials have been reluctant to challenge it, either inside or outside the boardrooms, but even under the terms of the 'social contract' with Harold Wilson and James Callaghan they have been reluctant to emerge outright as capitalist managers. And British capitalists and top managers see this too, for it is by being perceived as an opposition to 'management' that the trade unions can function as a rest-raining influence on shop-floor irresponsibility. The going schemes, then, have all had the problems of being tokenistic devices of cooptation, whose blatancy is itself a menace to stability.

The 'Scientific' Management of Men and Machines

F. W. Taylor articulated the dominant tough-minded ideo-logy of capitalist discipline in *Principles of Scientific Manage-ment* (1911) (New York, 1967), although 'The TaylorSystem' only brings to fruition the schemes of such as Bentham, Arkwright and Ure. Taylor takes the coercive politics of the capitalist industrial situation for granted; he does not raise general questions about the conditions of production but operates within the assumption of a boss having, through the threat of the sack and the promise of promotion, power over the worker, whose function it is to contribute to the boss's profit. This power means that the worker can be made to move at the boss's command, to surrender political agency at the gate and to function simply as, in Marx's words, 'an appendage to a machine'. Naturally idle and refractory, motivated by hunger or ambition, the worker is seen as a benthamoid moron, a goat, or pig, or ox, to whom productive activity could be nothing but a means to a selfish end. Such people, therefore, require supervision and co-ordination by company auxiliaries. But, especially through the organisation and rhythm of the machinery itself, an organisation which presents itself, once instituted, as technical, impersonal, objective and hence beyond politics, the worker's, misery could be welcomed as a spur to diligence or lamented as an inevitable by-product of modern times. Politics, however, were not far from the minds of the fathers of modern industrialism: Adam Smith, advancing the virtues of the division of labour, emphasised as one of the chief among them the prevention of 'sauntering about' between jobs *(Wealth of the Nations,* Pelican, p. 112). Andrew Ure, the philosopher of manufacture, had these things to say about the technological politics of spinning:

> Enlarging the spinning frame has recently given an extraordinary stimulus to mechanical science. In doubling the size of the mule, the owner is able to get rid of indifferent or restive spinners, and to become once more master of his mill, which is of no small advantage.

> This invention (the self-acting mule) confirms the great doctrine already propounded, that when capital enlists science in her service, the refractory hand of labour will always be taught docility. (Andrew Ure, *The Philosophy of Manufacture,* London 1835, (reprinted 1967) (pp. 365, 368)

The tasks of the worker, then, in keeping with his refractoriness, his inertia, and his stupidity and waywardness are, happily, able to be orchestrated for maximum discipline, speed, efficiency, and predictability under the control of owners and managers whose imagination and will are to be blindly and obediently carried out on the shop floor. What is

more, the dividing up of labour means that the atomic units of
motion to be repeated through time by the operatives can be
measured on a unitary work-calculus, enabling the employer
to know what a job is 'worth'. This aspect is brought out
clearly by Hannah Arendt in the context of distinguishing
modern division of labour from specialisation, with which it
is frequently identified:

> Yet, while specialisation of work is essentially guided by the
> finished product itself, whose nature it is to require different
> skills which are then pooled and organised together, division of
> labour, on the contrary, presupposes the qualitative equival-
> ence of all single activities for which no special skill is required,
> and these activities have no end in themselves, but actually
> represent only certain amounts of labour power which are
> added together in a purely quantitative way. (*The Human
> Condition*, Doubleday Anchor 1959, p. 107)

Managers, then, do not so much belong under the division
of labour as they belong over it, for they remain 'specialists'
in the arts of industrial statesmanship. It is they and their
higher technical assistants who supposedly infuse the industrial process with ideas, with that rationality that is supposed to mark off the human species as a whole. The workforce, meanwhile, and this includes those clerks whose rows
of typewriters and adding-machines accurately express the
mechanical nature of their 'mental' tasks, has the function of
mindlessly executing these ideas. Their work has no joy or
meaning save that which can be brought in from outside in
the form of competitive games or gestures of rebellion.
Productive activity, mankind's dominant and potentially one
of its most rewarding activities, functions for the alienated
labourer under capitalism as a means to a 'living', as a means
to the 'avoidance of pain'. The brutishness of all this is
explicit in Taylor, whose original paradigm at the Bethlehem
Steelworks was one 'Schmidt', 'a man of the type of the ox'.
(Harry Braverman's *Labour and Monopoly Capital*, Month-
ly Review Press, 1974, gives a good account of the centrality
of the Taylor System and, despite the shortcomings noted by
Braverman, so does Daniel Bell's chapter 'Work and its
Discontents' in *The End of Ideology*, Free Press, 1960. More

recently *The Division of Labour,* edited by André Gorz,
Harvester Press, 1976, treats many of the issues.)

We have noted the way statist thought presents 'society' as
lacking grass-root resources of self-control, as needing,
therefore, a quasi-external agency whose function it is precisely to fill this lack, as if you could speak of the 'essence' of
the Vice Squad as being to battle against vice. And the same
hierarchical dualism is operative here; workers are treated as
discrete instruments with an underling's measure of stupidity
and selfish greed the better that they might (through the
beneficent agency of entrepreneurial capitalists) be brought
from their natural torpor into productive activity. Thus must
the worker be a subject and thus it must be that it is only *qua*
consumer that he is 'sovereign', investing his energies in the
appropriation of such instruments of comfort and prestige as
his pay-packet allows, and enjoying through the vicarious
fantasy of television the freedom, power, expertise, and
artistry that is denied to him in the productive process. To
beneficiary and victim alike, then, the capitalist productive
hierarchy and the Taylor system which is still its most
representative articulation has acquired the status of what
Marx called 'a condition of nature'.

The Corporation as Benevolent Despot

Nonetheless, especially as people have always shown a
curious reluctance to be called to heel, the humanist wing of
liberalism has always flapped with concern at the dangerous
excesses of capitalist organisation. J.S. Mill, in his famous
added chapter 'The probable future of the labouring classes'
in *The Principles of Political Economy,* wrote:

> To work at the bidding and profit of another, without any
> interest in the work - the price of their labour being fixed by
> hostile competition, one side demanding as much and the other
> side paying as little as possible - is not, even when wages are
> high, a satisfactory state to human beings of educated intellig-
> ence, who have ceased to think of themselves as naturally
> inferior to those whom they serve. (Routledge, 1891, p.503)

And the less expensive commonsense recipe of Mrs.
Beeton predates the achievements of a hundred years of

'industrial relations' psychology:

> The sensible master and the kind mistress know, that if servants depend on them for their means of living, in their turn they are dependent on their servants for many of the comforts of life; and that with the proper amount of care in choosing servants, treating them like reasonable beings, and making slight excuses for the shortcomings of human nature, they will, save in some exceptional cases, be tolerably well served, and in most instances, surround themselves with attached domestics. (*Book of Household Management,* Third edition, 1888, p. 1454)

But British industrial politics have remained overwhelmingly despotic, reducing working-class struggle to predominantly defensive and disruptive oppositionism. Alarmed at the end of the First World War by the prospect of mass disloyalty to the industrial *status quo,* Government committees urged that workers be diverted from 'irresponsibility' by being given 'responsibility' within enterprises. And this is the growing wisdom to-day - to 'involve us all' in rescuing British capitalism. The owners of old paid no heed to the reformers and proceeded to take on the militants and beat the working class into submission. Since then, 'mistrust the masses' has been the dominant slogan implicit in British industry, as evidenced by the wholly hierarchical organisation even of the nationalised industries. To-day, despite gestures toward industrial democracy and more serious attempts by Tony Benn and by the Bullock Committee, it is fairly apparent that anti-democratic tendencies run deep in the English order, to the extent that for some time the stick of unemployment is going to be seen as a more manageable managerial weapon than the carrot of industrial enfranchisement. Revans, for example, commenting on the lack of response from managerial (or trade union) quarters to the meliorist suggestions of the Commission on Industrial Relations during the first Wilson government, notes:

> The long tradition of prerogatives, of authority descending in all its aspects and at all times without qualification and without question from those in nominal command, is so deeply rooted in British, indeed in Western culture, that the Commission speaks a language that the majority of managers do not

understand. (O.E.C.D. Report, p. 10)

We have seen that the Taylor System operates with a
Benthamite 'workhouse' picture of human motivation, seeing social activity as painful exertion undertaken for the sake
of private rewards extrinsic and antithetical to the work
activity itself. From our point of view it is interesting that
within managerial literature the most important criticisms of
'scientific management' have involved an attack on this
philosophical underpinning, emphasising with Mill and Beeton that working life should not be seen merely as people's
means of earning a wage with which to satisfy needs but
should itself be viewed as a place where human needs can be
either fulfilled or frustrated. Thus, whereas Taylor could do
nothing but fume, bribe, and bully in the face of workers'
refusal to beat to his time or march to his motion, the liberal
wing of management-theory has long urged bosses to adapt
their enterprises to the 'human needs of their employees and
thus create a harmony of interests within the factory. And so,
as different managerial schools debate, it is in the name of
different philosophies of human nature that they present and
interpret their findings, while hastening to stress the profitability to employers of a correct philosophy.

Elton Mayo and his associates, between 1927 and 1932,
carried out efficiency studies in Western Electric's Hawthorne Works in Chicago, studies which undermined 'scientific management' from within its own productivity goals and
which contested the basic philosophy of work propagated by
Taylor and espoused at large by management. The Hawthorne findings are well known: over a period of experimental manipulation of 'material' variables such as lighting
and wage-incentives it was found that productivity continued
to rise even when such material conditions were worsened.
Mayo attributed the improvement to the social atmsphere
generated by the experiment itself, and particularly to the
fact that workers saw the experiment as communicating a
concern for them 'as people' (the 'Hawthorne effect').
Moreover, within the experimental group, over a time,
informal group relationships among the operatives developed, along with a measure of job-control entailed in co-op-

erating with the investigators in their experimental design. In short, the experiment turned the workplace into a place of some co-operative fulfilment, into something other than a necessary grind, and the lesson was drawn that, if bosses would imitate Mayo's team and visibly perceive their workers as people, their concern would be reciprocated by the happy and loyal workforce (for a full report, see F.J. Roethlisberger and William J. Dickson *Management and the Worker,* Harvard,1939). Now Mayo's findings did not simply force themselves on a naive empirical investigator. Indeed, despite their unprecedented thoroughness, the Hawthorne studies have been criticised, by Alex Carey for example (*American Sociological Review,* 1967), for failing to advertise such things as their deliberate creation of a 'tame' experimental group; a group, in consequence, whose development of cohesion and identity would tend to be in terms of the corporation, not in terms of their class position. Hence the issue of class conflict was simply sidetracked.

A follower of the normative corporatism of Durkheim and the adaptive psychology of Janet, Mayo addressed himself in his major writings (*The Human Problems of an Industrial Civilisation.* 1933, *The Social Problems of an Industrial Civilisation,* 1945 (Routledge) and *The Psychology of Pierre Janet,* 1947) to the question of human life and work in an age of the destruction of 'all the historic social and personal relationships' (*Social Problems,* p. 8) and their replacement at the core of social organisation by the big firm and the state. Bereft of clear statuses and clear duties, the historically created masses of mutually anxious and hostile individuals were consumed by spiritual sickness, unable to find satisfaction in work, and prone to be swept up in 'pathological' quests for 'substitute' gratification in national or class militancy. Curiously, while constantly emphasising the competitive market and the profit motive as the source of the ills he vividly depicts, Mayo, with equal and comic constancy, presented workers' 'attributing ills to a hostile world' (*Social Problems,* p. 27) as symptomatic of their pathological obsessions. (Catch 23: capitalism drives people mad; the chief symptom of this madness is hostility to capitalism.) Mayo saw that orthodox industrial organisation was pernicious, and insisted on a richer perspective on working life: 'Any industrial organisation is at once a way of working - which must be technically expert and effective - and also a way of living for many people a co-operative system which must be efficient, satisfactory as a way of living' (*Social Problems*, p. 49). In working out this theme Mayo broaches, often with great insight, many central issues of human social life. But he is an idealist. He never seeks answers below the level of 'consciousness', below the level of getting people to think of themselves as part of enterprises whose overall structure, technology, and purpose are left untouched. And so it is little wonder that Mayo's 'human relations school' has become associated with crass manipulation of the workforce and with the cheap gimmickry of corporate communalism - with the idea that a supervisory smile costs less than a wage rise or a new machine - or a rebellion. As a thin disguise of industrial reality, then, Human Relations has been attacked by those outraged by its deception as well as by those alarmed by its transparency. And, while managerial practice has tended away from Mayo's schemes, it is interesting that the major development in managerial thinking since Mayo has been the attempt to dig deeper into working life for the key to a happy marriage of fulfilment and productivity. Thus it is that we turn to the philosophy of 'job-enrichment'.

Labour as Fulfilment: Job-Enrichment

Mayo projected the idea that workers' problems were in their heads (as a psychology student I had to write an essay on 'accident proneness' as a 'personality trait'). Thus the development of 'human relations' industrial psychology has been the development of a network of spiritual props to bolster the worker's marriage to the firm. 'Job-enrichment' in its various forms seeks to break out from Mayo's mentalism and to emphasise the 'objective' 'sociotechnical situation' of the worker. Drawing on the moral psychologists John Dewey, Abraham Maslow and Eric Fromm, Jensis Likert, D. McGregor, Chris Argyris, Frederick Herzberg and others have argued that contrary to the traditional Benthamite-capitalist assumption that activity (production) is undertaken only as a means to pleasure or the reduction of pain (consumption), human beings are fundamentally active, creative, intellectual, decisive, problem-solving. Work, then, can and should be attractive, challenging, self-regulated, and involving. Thus for example, relative job-security, far from destroying motivation as is assumed in the Bentham-Taylor picture, tends to remove one basis of exhausting anxiety and disruptive resentment and so, given the right task-situation 'motivators', releases productive 'potential' to be 'tapped'. As Herzberg wrote: 'Idleness, indifference and irresponsibility are healthy responses to absurd work' (*Work and the Nature of Man,* World Publishing Co., 1966). Hence, merely to spray 'human relations' sentiment into the industrial atmosphere without doing away with the shit-work itself is not only pernicious, it is a waste of company resources. As Herzberg wrote in *Harvard Business Review* March/April 1969: 'Job-Enrichment Pays Off!'. (Other key texts are: D. McGregor: *The Professional Manager,* McGraw Hill, 1967; Chris Argyris: *Personality and Organisation,* Harper and Row, 1957; and Rensis Likert: *The Human Organisation.* There are extracts in *Management and Motivation* edited by V.H. Vroom and E.L. Deci, Penguin, 1970, and an excellent presentation of this whole outlook is the already mentioned *Work in America, Report of a Special Task Force to the Secretary of Health, Education, and Welfare,* M.I.T., 1973.)

The very hallmark of modern industry, the hierarchical division of unpleasant labour, is thus being examined by the administrators themselves. And this, whether or not it is intended merely as a shift in ruling-class tactics, entails a sharp break. The 'negativity' of work, Adam's curse, is implicit in Western-culture: work is a lifetime sacrificed, unless you are an 'artist' - or a 'philosopher' - and requires the bolstering, not only of the sanctions of penury, but of a 'work ethic' instilled from early childhood. 'Welfare' (faring well) has been twisted into a concept centring on consumption, while 'consumption' has itself turned into a concept centring on ownership: so that what we 'have' and its 'cost' are the marks of individual wellbeing. And, as Eli Chinoy's *Automobile Workers and the American Dream,* (Beacon, 1968) brings out, however much we honour a massive corporation with the label of 'free enterprise', freedom and enterprise consist, as far as their employees are concerned, in activities antithetical to their jobs: in hobbies, in a dreamed-of 'going it alone', and in the purchasing power provided through the drudgery of work. But such 'well-being' requires massive industrial output. And 'modern industry', for all its un-pleasantness, is what delivers the goods (and would you rather go back to the stone-age? etc.). The nature of modern work thus appears as a general instrumental necessity. So, as Alisdair Clayre ironically hints (*The Times, 1969*):

> Perhaps work is so inherently unpleasant that only coercion and an authoritarian relationship between appointed manager and hired hand can, in the long run, deal with it.

Certainly there are powerful currents in the socialist and Marxist streams that justify Clayre's question. These cur-rents, polluted by optimistic fatalism about 'modern tech-nology' see the abolition of scarcity as the condition of freedom and see the despotic accumulation of capital ('development') as the condition of that abolition. Moreover they see this development as an inevitable force in capitalist society and an overriding imperative in socialist society's 'earlier phase'. Thus they tend to avoid questions of the political technology (questions that are imposed within other Marxist currents stressing 'the social relations of production') and, whether wittingly or not, to embrace a technocratic authoritarianism. Against the 'anti-authoritarians', for example, Engels insisted that 'independent of all social organisation', 'the automatic machinery of a big factory is much more despotic than the small capitalists who employ workers have ever been ('On Authority', *Marx and Engels Selected Works* Vol 1, Moscow, 1962, p. 637), yet automatic machinery was not to be avoided or reformed. Lenin also contesting self-management tendencies, wrote in 1920:

> Socialism is inconceivable without the large-scale capitalist engineering based on the latest discoveries of modern science. It is inconceivable without planned state organisation which keeps tens of millions to the strictest observance of a unified standard in production and distribution... At the same time

socialism is inconceivable unless the proletariat is at the head of the state. ...Only the lackeys of the bourgeoisie would invite the workers to resist the Taylor system... (*Left Wing Childishness and Petty Bourgeois Mentality*, Moscow, 1973, pp. 19, 27)

The editor's footnote to the Taylor reference reads:

Taylor, Frederick Winslow, (1856-1915) - an American engineer who set up a system of labour organisation involving the rational application of tools and machinery and the elaboration of correct methods of work combined with increased demands on the workers. (p. 37)

More recently, Ernest Mandel, who like Engels, Lenin, Trotsky and Stalin, tends to dichotomise politics and productive technology: as if you can have socialism and workers' power when the workers' work-situation is itself one of ignorance and powerlessness, argues against ('petty bourgeois') advocates of devolution:

Experience has made it quite clear that the fundamental tendency of modern technology... is to move towards a centralisation and socialisation of labour... (this) makes possible a radical reduction in the working week and the gradual disappearance of alienating mechanical labour once capitalism has been overthrown. ('Workers' Control and Works Councils' I.M.G. Pamphlet, 1972)

For Mandel, then, it is sufficient to point to technology's own tendency and to hail the social spin-off from that process; there is little 'tendency' to see the extent to which apparently technical questions need to be politically unpacked to reveal the issues of power lurking behind them and little concern that technological development has always had the 'tendency' it has had because of its place in the weaponry of class rule. (Stephen Marglin's article 'What do Bosses do?', *Review of Radical Political Economics,* Vol, 6, No. 2, 1974 (reprinted in *The Division of Labour*, ed. Andre Gorz, Harvester, 1976) explores this theme.)

Technology, then, appears, both to the left and to the right, as a given framework whose development is beyond argument. Hence, when Hugh Clegg writes that 'it is impossible for the workers to share directly in the management'

(*New Approach to Industrial Democracy,* p. 119), tendent-
iousness trots out as truism, the 'iron law of oligarchy'
parades as the modern human condition, and the lack of
interest among assembly-line workers, much advertised by
bureaucrats on 'both sides of industry', appears as a law of
industrial nature. If developed productive organisation is
inherently stifling, who could want the privilege of participat-
ing in its administration? The managerialists G. Strauss and
E. Rosenstein correctly write in 'Workers' Participation, a
Critical Review' (in *Industrial Relations,* University of California Publication, February 1970): 'In many production tech-
nologies it is difficult to provide direct, job-centred opport-
unities for participation' (p. 213). But this truth, rather than
bringing the political question to a close, should force the
technological question into the open.

What is 'job-enrichment, and how does it undermine the
managerial and technocratic ideology? Unlike 'worker participation', to be discussed further on, 'job-enrichment' specifically focuses on the way workers spend their work-time, in
their relationship to equipment and in relation to their
workmates. Capitalist factories in Sweden, Japan, the
U.S.A., Britain and Holland are experimenting in these
directions (*Work in America* contains an excellent summary
of these developments). It is also an aspect of the 'Chinese
road' (See Stuart Schram's *Authority, Participation and
Cultural Change,* Cambridge, 1974). I have already counter-
posed the 'philosophy' of 'job-enrichment' to that of 'scientific management', and this comes out in a detailed antithesis
at the practical level. Where Taylor prescribes simple tasks,
job enrichment indicates complex tasks; where Taylor prescribes minimising necessary skill, job-enrichment indicates
the development of skills; where Taylor prescribes repetition
job-enrichment indicates variation; where Taylor prescribes
task fragmentation, job-enrichment indicates task-holism;
where Taylor prescribes social fragmentation on the shop-
floor, job-enrichment indicates work-teams; where Taylor
prescribes the annihilation of individuality in production, job-
enrichment indicates its utilisation; where Taylor prescribes
supervision, job-enrichment indicates group self-discipline;

where Taylor prescribes the separation of plan and execution, job-enrichment indicates their integration; where Taylor prescribes centralisation, job-enrichment indicates devolution; where Taylor prescribes wage and status differentials, job-enrichment indicates wage and status equalisation; where Taylor prescribes mechanical determination of work-speeds, job-enrichment indicates worker determination of machine speeds; where Taylor prescribes mechanical routines for humans, job-enrichment indicates the automation of the mechanical. In short, a deeply dualistic structure is replaced by integration as a productive ideal.

Volvo in Sweden have built a £9 million automobile factory at Kalmar, designed on a 'cellular' rather than an 'assembly-line' system, with five assembly areas opening onto a central materials store. Supplied by automated trucks, twenty-man 'autonomous' teams each assemble a whole 'job', for example, the electrical system. Teams are responsible for their own organisation, machine maintenance, and quality-control, and can vary the pace of work within an overall plan agreed between the unions and the company. Rotation of work is encouraged within and among teams and workers take leave to study engineering at advanced levels. Plant installation costs, including facilities for the work teams, were higher than for a comparable assembly-line factory, but productivity, especially taking into account the drop in labour turnover and in production defects, is already at least as high as that in the more orthodox Volvo factories (For a succinct, but now somewhat outdated account, see *Motor*, 10th November 1973). Furukawa Electric Company in Japan manufactures a variety of electrical goods. There, a policy of 'anti-systematism' was introduced, involving among other things the abolition of specialist trainers, supervisors etc., and the taking over of many clerical functions by the 'autonomous' work-teams. Dozens of factories throughout the world, in fact, have abolished time-clocks, done away with canteen apartheid (still, of course, a virulent feature of the British university), and made semi-redundant such categories as time-keepers, foremen, inspectors and maintenance-staff. Workers are encouraged to develop a scientific understanding of advanced technology and to question and participate in the improvement of their work-conditions. And, over a short time, as catalogued in *Work in America,* the results, in sheer profit and loss terms for the company, have almost always been positive.

Despite this record, harped on by institutes and foundation think-tanks, 'job-enrichment' is not popular. Of course, although not emphasised by the American prophets, the enrichment of work entails big outlay on plant and equipment if it is to be anything more than 'human relations' with brass knobs on. But new factories are being built in any case, so this cannot be the explanation. For all its appeal to 'will' Revans' O.E.C.D. pamphlet exposes, perhaps, the main point:

> Our problem is not in a lack of ideas, nor of methods. Least of all is it in a lack of need. What is missing is the will to try: the threat to established hierarchies of power in seeking the help, advice and support of those who traditionally do what they are told to do, is still too great to be faced. For even if new attitudes to authority were developed out of such cooperation, the basic conflict of interest remains: 'How are the benefits of our co-operation to be shared out?'... The question is, in itself, unavoidable and on that account most managements still prefer to argue it on the existing battlefield they know so well'. (p. 120)

At the factory level alone, 'job-enrichment' entails apparently drastic reforms. Job-enrichers invite salaried managers to promote their own redundancy by initiating integrated production methods in the interests of a corporate 'team' that does not yet exist - little wonder that its appeal in the company offices is limited. Job-enrichers invite elite specialist or supervisory workers, whose differential status is a prime concern of Clive Jenkins' A.S.T.M.S. to abandon or share their functions and skills - little wonder that the 1973 T.U.C. Interim Report *Industrial Democracy* warns that job-enrichment 'may be regarded by supervisors as a threat to their status' (p. 30). Job-enrichers invite trade-union officials to cut across the very divisions that maintain their power in order to foster a direct job control unmediated by full-time union officers - little wonder they are not enthused. Job-enrichers invite rank and file workers to abandon their indifference or hostility to their work and to give up the painfully developed defence-tactic of the work-to-rule and the demarcation dispute for the prospect of a more satisfying working day in the service of the same old bosses (or the new ones that buy the old ones out) - little wonder that most workers express scepticism at the idea of a radically different working life.

For all its promise of the happy capitalist factory then, the job-enrichment movement is seen as a threat or a fantasy by its putative beneficiaries. Yet, by highlighting the alterable miseries of shop-floor life, by exposing the waste and inefficiency of capitalism's bureaucratic hierarchy, and by throwing up viable alternatives, it has thrown the political dimension of management into relief, subverting from within the idea of co-ordination and atomisation as purely technical imperatives of advanced production. What emerges is that the more work is divided from above the more it needs to be ruled from above and that the more work is ruled from above the more it needs to be divided from above; despotism and atomisation are mutually reinforcing. The job-enrichment movement, moreover, brings out the political dimension of technology as an aspect of productive organisation, stripping off its natural-because-physical, objective-because-scientific, veneer. Capitalist technology, as Adam Smith and Andrew Ure knew long ago, shapes and rivets power relations at the point of production. Its evolution, in turn, is by no means an automatic process, but expresses those power relations; most obviously it is the capitalists and their managers who fund research and choose its results for their own purposes. Capitalist technology no more 'ignores' human beings than does a slave-driver's whip; both the 'scientific manager' and the 'job-enricher' bring a 'philosophy of man' into the situation they are trying to control. And so, although techno-drudgery has been transmitted as though ordained by scientific law, the politics of technocratic science, (which has always sought to assist the 'prediction and control' of certain humans by other humans apparently aloof from the 'system' on which they operate) is brought into relief by a movement for which managerial 'attitudes' constitute not so much a given perspective as an obstacle to progress. Job-enrichment throws into relief the authoritarian mystery-mongering of science as a justifier of the capitalist order; whereas a monopoly of control is traditionally presented as a requirement of science, the monopoly of science now appears as a requirement of control, and collective involvement in scientific work and the collective use of its results can be seen as a condition of advanced production. Technological fatalists of left and right, technocrat and anti-technocrat, have scant excuse for extrapolating from the tyrannical Western/Soviet experience. Factory despotism is no more natural than slavery; and slavery once seemed the most natural thing in the world.

Job-enrichment's protest against capitalist tradition strikes home precisely because it develops within the capitalist seminaries (such as the Massachussetts Institute of Technology) themselves. After all, the whole rationale of the movement has been to provide such 'motivation' as will reconcile the pursuit of happiness of workers with the pursuit of stable profits by the firm, to achieve:

> ... the removal of barriers to collaboration and the reconciliation of both efficiency and social satisfaction within the ambit of common purpose provided by the goals of the enterprise. (J. Child, *British Management Thought,* Allen and Unwin, 1969, p. 118)

These fundamental attacks on the elitism of standard managerial ideology (Argyris likes to point to the success of mentally defective people on production-lines) do not emanate from irresponsible anarchists or leftists. Indeed, as I have already stressed, it is to save the Church that the religion has been attacked. McGregor and Herzberg think that alienation is a function of the work-activity itself; without argument they restrict their reforming zeal to the shop-floor and urge little change at top-management level. In their writings I found scant reference to the idea of a fundamental antagonism between worker and employer, nor any investigation of the significance of ownership for the direction of managerial responsibility. Vigorously exposing the micro-politics of the classical factory they do not even question the power of capital, let alone its impact on the detail of factory life. Assuming a potential coincidence of interest between the enrichment of jobs and the enrichment of proprietors, these writers simply by-pass the structural implications of capital for work. Thus they do not consider the possibility that managerial authoritarianism can only be understood in the light of the need to subdue those to whom the accumulation of capital and the appropriation of profit is inimical. Thus, basing their findings on experiments with workers whose 'problem' is typically one of boredom, dropping out, poor workmanship, and absenteeism, they present job-enrichment to the capitalists as a panacea for industrial trouble. It is as if elections for policemen were offered as the solution to urban crime. And this is true of all the participatory remedies now being canvassed, from job-enrichment to worker-directorships. Professor Revans' O.E.C.D. report embodies the incoherence of the new capitalist philanthropy:

> In our present concern for participation we must never forget that management must still retain the task of proposing what the participation is to be about: management proposals may well be changed, both by the velocity of external events and by the very process of negotiation, but management's prime responsibility can never be abandoned, much less usurped. Even if management is further democratised it must, like any democratic government, be clear what its own desired policy is. (p. vi)

So workers are to 'democratically' submit to what is, in any case, decided over their heads. The conceptual collision in the democratic-despotic position well expresses the conflict within the industrial situation itself, a conflict recognised by the British Institute of Personnel Management in its 1974 conference on worker participation. For fear of 'loss of capital to the company' the Conference agreed that workers 'may share in the discussion of operational targets but not major decision-making' and that company books should be kept away from the lower orders (Unpublished Conference Report). While capitalists and bosses may need the cooperation that job-enrichment and other participatory schemes promise, they can have this cooperation only by creating conditions which endanger it. The more the function of 'management' is devolved the more deeply are the battle-lines of class struggle drawn into capitalist territory. There, top-management and its bureaucracy would appear less and less as technically essential coordinators of production and more and more as the executive committee of the 'controlling interest', as coercive agents of capitalist control. And this structural confrontation would sit uneasily alongside the democratic slogans of 'participation and enrichment'.

As we have seen, it is not for their intrinsic value that satisfaction or involvement of workers is a concern of capitalist industrial relations policy. Capitalist industry functions for its owners' profit. Paying and in other ways pacifying the labour force which makes that profit possible are costs to the company, of which the workers are not members. The satisfaction or dissatisfaction of the worker do not appear on its balance-sheet any more than do the enhancement or ruination of the factory's surroundings (pollution caused by a factory is not part of company costs). It may be necessary to ameliorate workers' conditions in order to increase 'worker input' and decrease all kinds of costs and risks. But this amelioration is itself costly and carries with it the well advertised risks of Giving an Inch. The steps, then, are a debit which only increased profitability can counterbalance. There is no direct common interest here between the worker and his employer (user); improved conditions, like higher wages, are forced on the employer and will be taken away by him if it suits him and if he can get away with it. And as companies struggle to survive in the semi-defoliated jungle which is contemporary capitalism, there is nothing like the speed-up or the sack to shatter the illusions of creative teamwork so eagerly fostered by managerial liberals. For, not only are workers subject to their own capitalist employers, they are subject to market fluctuations which can deprive them of their livelihood at a financier's signature. And, whereas, according to the divine rule that to him that hath shall be given, the shrewd capitalist's selectively promiscuous investments will, assuming the system is not upset by civil commotion, generally leave him and his loved ones well looked after in case he has to close or sell a factory, the worker is right out of a job. Moreover, the very threat implicit in this invidious situation is itself the key to the capitalist's hold over the worker in the factory.

Whatever temperature-controls operate within the factory, then, it is subject to the floods, droughts, and blizzards of the capitalist market and to those with the most powerful position in that market, the international ruling class. Now, survival in that class requires more than the ownership of labour; it requires, for example, minimum investment and maximum product-turnover. So, as well as conditioning what is produced, the market shapes how well it is produced and dictates that at least as much is spent on tarting up and advertising the commodity as on making it. And so, bringing the 'realities of the outside world' back to the cosy and democratically enriched work-situation as envisaged by Herzberg and his fellows, we are invited to contemplate the fulfilled worker earnestly, creatively, and freely producing, if not utter junk, then goods designed to become junk with the lapse of a decent interval. The producer is supposed to take pride in being responsible for making what, as a consumer, he holds in contempt, to find meaning in the production of what he knows to be pointless; to find his soul in the very act of selling it.

The job-enrichers are trying to foster responsible participation in an inherently irresponsible system. They do not see that that system depends on fragmenting and bureaucratising the productive process so that no one accepts responsibility for its nature and consequences: the bosses protected by 'the necessities of business', the rank-and-file by 'just following orders'. Our capitalist reformers, then, might find embarrassing the tendency of workers once involved in the total activity of production, to take their 'responsibilities' seriously. In 1976, for example, Lucas Combine's Shop Stewards' Committee began urging the British company to embark on 'socially useful' lines of production rather than to cut production and jobs in line with current market trends. *Labour Research* (March 1976), reports:

Of course, the Corporate Plan says, no company can be

transformed into an 'island of responsibility and concern in a sea of irresponsibility and depravity'. However, the Corporate Plan is an attempt to question the assumptions on which the firm operates and is a contribution to the movement for greater control by workers over their working lives. (pp. 63-4)

Much more radical was the activity of the Builders Labourers Federation in Sydney, Australia where $3,000,000,000 worth of 'development' (destruction) was held up around 1972 by workers determined to control not only their conditions of work but the content of that work. Through 'green bans' the unionists prevented the destruction by developers of working-class communities, parkland and historic buildings.

One of the things at issue through all this is the substance of what we mean by 'responsibility'. And the tensions in word-drift here reflect different working ethics. The 'responsible' labourer of capitalism's classic phase was Ure's obedient labourer, held by the abstract dutifulness of 'Christian' piety or Utilitarian patience to his task. Job-enrichers and other participationists have sought a higher form of internal discipline: the worker is to be brought to love his firm and his work and hence to respond to the company's needs. (Idleness and counter-manipulation are fitting reactions to such heteronomy.) Workers who go beyond these to seek to exercise responsibility for the conditions in which they and those who live with their products will live, who have developed an autonomous responsiveness, are still considered the irresponsibles. No Government Committee has yet proposed a mode of incorporating productive freedom—though, as we shall now see, the Bullock Committee almost conjures up the appearance of such alchemy.

Orchestrated Democracy: The Bullock Report and British Industry

British workers' 'oppositionism' has, as I have suggested, made progress toward industrial democracy difficult: 'let them be the bosses; don't let them grind you down'. At the same time, however, this 'oppositionism' shows itself in a long tradition of sophisticated and militant resistance to capitalist regimentation - having fought 'productivity-deals' in the late 1960s, for example, workers turned the employers' strategy on its head by forcing large wage increases. All this makes the incorporation of workers, their cooptation into 'the enterprise', an overwhelming problem. Following Sir Robert Carr's 'Fair Deal at Work', which in turn followed Barbara Castle's abortive 'In Place of Strife', the Heath Government offered considerable 'advantages' to trade union hierarchies if they would be prepared to take on the role of state-certified power-brokers. But these offers of legitimacy came at a time of intense strife in the place and of bitter awareness of raw deals at work. Thus they presented the union officials with the prospect of blessings from above at the cost of curses from below and a consequent loss of legitimacy as 'representatives' of working people. 'Moderate' Joe Gormley, for example, had either to emerge as a (Tory) bosses' man or 'lead' the miners in bringing down the Heath Government. There followed Harold Wilson's 'Social Contract', an event of Lockean obscurity, in which trade unon officials gained tremendous informal power and came to be seen as quasi-legitimate 'politicians' in their own right. In a climate of recession, and mobilised despair, a sullen acquiescence prevailed for three years as workers were persuaded to rock neither the National nor the Labour Party boats. (Contract: if you keep us going, we will keep going.) Meanwhile, however, despite obliging attempts in the media to depict them as bolshevik wolves, the officials' legitimacy as representatives was being eroded by the simple fact that they were 'voluntarily' presiding over a systematic attack on their members' 'inflated' living standards and 'privileged' working conditions. It is this erosion, as far as I can see, in a context of unwillingness to desert the capitalist state's 'volunteer force', that explains the sudden switch of the T.U.C. 'majority' to back the hitherto rejected idea of 'participation', and to recommend, through their involvement in the 'majority' Bullock Report, a scheme whereby they might re-establish their links with the shop-floor, albeit links of a quasi-managerial kind.

The Report of the Committee of Inquiry on Industrial Democracy, (chaired by Oxford committee-man/historian,

Lord Alan Bullock and published by H.M. Government in
January 1977), is divided into a 'main' and minority sections
(the majority line 'going too far' for the Committee's
capitalist members). The 'majority' report presents the need
for 'industrial democracy' primarily on the difficulties that
large corporations exerience in gaining shop-floor
acceptance of the need for 'flexibility' in a context of
'technological change and rapid fluctuations in the economic
climate'. They 'therefore' restrict their recommendations to
firms with more than 2,000 employees.

> Often their (senior management's) decisions closely affect the
> lives of thousands of employees, and in such cases it becomes
> increasingly difficult for employers to deny the right of their
> employees, not only to have their interests taken into account
> by management, but also to have an opportunity for active
> involvement in the decision-making process. Such responses
> on the part of companies may in part be a recognition of social
> responisbility or of democratic principles, but they are also
> evidence of the practical reality that if a company neglects to
> make provision for such involvement, employees are now in a
> position, through the strengthening of trade union
> organisation and power to resist the implementation of
> changes that threaten their livelihood and security. (p. 21)

Aware of the strategic uselessness of mere tokenism, the
majority report confronts this problem boldly. It urges,
contrary to the drift of *Work in America* that
'job-enrichment' without 'democratisation' of the 'overall
authority structure in the firm' can do no more than
ameliorate working life within 'extremely narrow' limits and
'at worst' functions as a mere 'technique' for engineering
acquiescence (p. 46). It recommends that 'workers'
representatives' should sit down with the 'shareholders'
representatives' (established senior management) on the
Board of Directors itself rather than on the pedestal of
'supervisory boards' on the 'European model', originating in
1937 Germany, wherein policy-making functions are left
firmly in established hands. It recommends a change in
company law so that firms would have 'responsibilities' for
the well-being of their workforce as well as for the
enrichment of their shareholders. Clearly these would be

major reforms, whose magnitude reflects the Bullock diagnosis of British industry as being ground to a halt by managerial born-to-rule authoritarianism and proleterian work-to-rule bloody-mindedness. An examination of the recommendations reveals, I think, that it is only by contrast with the Divine Right absolutism of capitalist industrial rule that the Bullock Report's William-and-Mary solutions could be thought of as either glorious or revolutionary.

Who are to be 'the workers' representatives?' (given that the majority of a firm's employees vote through the proposed secret ballot that they do want to be 'represented' at all?) They are to be union members, 'generally' employees of the company, 'selected' by an 'appropriate method' by the 'recognised trade unions in the company' (p. 118). Shop stewards and convenors are envisaged as the front-runners in the worker-director race (those same shop stewards whom the 1968 Donovan Report on industrial relations, a report in which the notion of 'industrial democracy' played no part, singled out as, despite their 'image', crucial 'oil' in the industrial-relations machinery). Non-unionists are to be out of the picture, a suggestion which has provoked disingenuous protest from the populists of the Confederation of British Industry and one which puts a premium on union membership. This trade-union dominance, it seems clear, is the pivot of the T.U.C. shift. For, as I have suggested, it is at plant level that trade union organisation and control of its members has been eroded as complicity in wage-cuts and sackings eroded its shop-floor support. From the unions' viewpoint, then, Bullock's function is to recapture official control of the workforce by enabling union officials to work in ameliorist ways within the managerial framework of individual companies.

If workers are not to elect their 'representatives', Bullock envisages only tenuous contact thereafter. No provision is made for 'worker directors' to spend any time on the shop floor, or to return there after their term of office. No provision is made whereby the workforce can recall their 'representatives' or otherwise directly control those who act in their name. Rather, it is the selecting union officials who are explicitly named as the 'constituents' and, provided they act unanimously, given the right to sack 'worker directors' (p. 122). Who is representing whom? Moreover, being legally obliged to act on behalf of 'the firm as a whole', 'worker directors' cannot legally be mandated from below. 'Sensitive' matters are still (by law) able to be voted 'confidential' to Board members, further separating them from those outside. Yet, urging that 'representatives' 'report back' and 'keep in touch' with the shop floor, the Report insists that 'too close identification with management and loss of confidence of those they represent' is 'not inevitable'.

Assuming, contrary to envisaged fact, that the 'representatives' were indeed representatives, what would happen to them in the Boardroom? Well, they would be equal in number with shareholders' 'representatives' (fair enough?) but must, with them, co-opt an odd number further group: (2X Y). The third group is expected to be made up of:

> ... the best among those who are at present non-executive directors; senior personnel from other companies;... solicitors, bankers, accountants and so on; of local and national trade union officials... . (p. 97)

(Should a deadlock arise over cooptation, the aptly titled 'Industrial Democracy Commission' will step in and sort things out.) The formula, then, ensures minority status for the 'worker directors' - all have parity, but some have more parity than others. While the prudence of 'communication' is urged on the bosses, no rule is envisaged requiring them to divulge vital information to their junior partners on the Board.

A British Labour Government Report, even one too radical to be implemented, is not going to attack capitalism, whether in its private or state form. The Bullock Report is, in a way analogous to the job-enrichment philosophy of *Work in America,* radical in its insistence on 'real' change and in its genuine challenge of capitalist absolutist ideology. Yet, as I have suggested, it would be quite wrong to think of it as a blueprint for 'industrial democracy'. Rather, it is an attempt to institutionalise the notion of a 'common interest' between labour and capital, controller and controlled, with the message that firms exist to serve both, and through the medium of the common managerial interests of trade unions officials and established company directors. In stressing this, I am taking issue with those who defend Bullock's trade union orientation in terms of the militant traditions and power-resources of trade unions, and who argue that the workers outside the union structure are helpless dupes of capital. Such defences, it seems to me, share the conservative fantasy of an essentially ductile workforce whose loyalty is threatened only by outside agitators. This ignores both the inherent dynamics of class struggle and class initiative and the role of trade unions in stifling and segmenting that struggle and initiative. Certainly there are historical currents that flow into newly developing institutions of producers' power, and the implementation of Bullock would in practice promote this process as the gap between what it deems and what it effects becomes critically clear. Bullock offers an expensive token whose relation to what it is a token of is likely to be too close for the comfort either of bosses or bureaucrats.

Towards Democratic Industry

General democracy under capitalism, then, is a utopian aspiration. There are many levels to the politics of work, and all these levels interlock. Accordingly, the road to industrial democracy is complex. You cannot single out 'worker directorships' as the secret of industrial enfranchisement. You cannot prescribe 'nationalisation' as the instrument of industrial equality. You cannot single out 'job-enrichment' as the key to industrial freedom. Working people could and should direct industry, but the 'worker director' principle, even shorn, as in workers' cooperatives, of its usual trade-union-official interpretation, leaves alone both the capitalist market and the capitalist division of labour. It is a blueprint for cooptation. Production is not properly a 'private' matter and should be brought under the control of the public who do it and who must live off its fruits, good and bad. But nationalisation by a State apparatus geared to centralist hierarchy in general and to capitalism in particular leaves alone the subordinate position of workers and the passive isolation of society's members; 'public ownership'

to-day means private control by bureaucrats at public
expense - it is a blueprint for statism. People should and
could find pleasure and fulfilment in the needed activity
which takes up and will foreseeably continue to take up so
much of their lives; but 'job-enrichment' leaves top
management and its profit-oriented rule alone. It is a
blueprint for pacification. And all this remains true despite
the fact that all these moves from above imply fundamental
retreats by our rulers and imply fundamental questioning of
capitalist structures.

A free, just, and democratic society would have to
overturn capitalist structures at every level. If we reject the
technocratic rationale of the division of labour, we ought to
subvert divisions between rulers and ruled, between experts
and ignoramuses, between skilled and unskilled, between
men's work and women's work. And this means not only
lowering barriers between different social functions, tearing
down the corrals that keep apart electricians, farmers,
intellectuals, doctors, garbage collectors, clerks, and
politicians, but breaking down barriers between 'the
workers' and 'the community'. In part this is a question of
opening up factories in a quite physical sense, as the Lipp
workers did in France in 1973-4. But it is more than this: it
means approaching the abolition of 'worker' as a special
category of people. At present, for example' children,
housewives, and old people, not to mention academics, are
cut off from social production, trapped in schools, homes,
and 'homes', and are mean t to be grateful to be away
from the 'rough and tumble' of industry. These divisions
damage all, retarding child development, rendering useless
the old, imprisoning the housewife, while perpetuating the
horrors of industry by localising and hiding it, and by tearing
apart production and consumption. They become
unnecessary where the ways of working are geared to the
working people themselves. Though different, then, division
of labour and specialisation are subject to a common critique.
As defined by Arendt, the division of labour, the breakdown
of a work process into measurable atoms, each the task of one
labourer, is a phenomenon specific to the micro-politics of
the capitalist factory-floor. But from another point of view it

is paradigmatic of the sort of social splitting that specialisation also represents. For, if division of labour entails the control by managerial mind over operative matter, a society of specialists, as Plato in *The Republic* shows, is a society of the mutually ignorant, who thus stand in need of direction by a know-all, a specialist in generality. Thus the philosopher-king, thus the Civil Service, and thus the Kremlin bureaucracy with its self-promoting story that the 'Scientific-Technological Revolution' will, under its guidance, both increase specialisation and enhance social equality. Some hope. (See *A Worker in a Worker's State*, Miklos Haraszti, Penguin, 1977.)

To advocate 'workers' power' without clarifying the category 'worker' is to invite confusion. I am not thinking only of the issue of whether housewives are 'members of the working class'. If, for example, we think of 'workers' as a genus embracing a multiplicity of distinct species, we shall tend to think in terms of the radically divided and sectionalised workforce that we now have. And if we then raise the question of what it means to speak of workers' power in that circumstance, we shall have to consider how such a workforce, with its differentiated conditions, responsibilities, and powers, based on different locations in the political economy, is to exercise 'that power'. We then have to face the imbalances, conflicts, and actual and potential injustices of this situation. This may be inevitable but, unless the tendency is there to move beyond this inheritance from feudalism and capitalism, we can discern 'The Workers' State' with 'general and public good' as its special and private concern looming up as the superior solver of these conflicts; with 'bureaucratic degeneration' built into its very constitution. We have seen in the discussion of 'job-enrichment' that hierarchy and division feed on one another, so that only to the extent that 'community' exists as a practical reality can such reproduction of capitalist relations be eroded. And this means a radical breakdown of hierarchy and specialisation. This can partially be achieved by rotating jobs, which handles the question 'who will pick up the garbage', as well as educating people and, as the Chinese communists say, broadening their outlook. But modern technology contains the potential for much more than this. Cybernetic production makes rewarding kinds of work at a controllable scale possible. It requires, moreover, an understanding of general principles ('systems theory', etc.). This means that a person educated to work in one area is equipped to operate in diverse fields. And so, if scientific activity is liberated by the community from the strategic preserves of academies and institutes, it is able to function as a radicalising, democratising, and liberating force of production. When all workers need to be scientists, scientific elitism becomes a fetter and technocratic mystery-mongering becomes difficult. What is called our 'education system' functions at present as a device for excluding those whose culture does not conform to the bookish discipline demanded of the career-cream of managerial capitalism. As such it serves to prepare a 'labour supply' ready-tamed, ready-graded ('failure' to 'flier'), directly perpetuating social division and legitimating the process in terms of 'objective' assessments of peoples—if the working-class boy is thick, after all, he can hardly aspire to emulate or overturn his betters. Democratic work-politics could hardly fail to include an attack on our school system and could not fail to liberate children from the all-day routines of 'school work' that they may learn from a wider experience as direct observers and as direct participants in the productive life of the community.

I have stressed the political dangers of specialisation, of professionalism, of the situation where the possession of a specialised skill or body of knowledge, maintained though an active system of education and certification, makes possible the control and exploitation by some of others and generates an overall culture of servile and mystified ignorance. But the 'attack' on specialisation itself must be balanced by an awareness of the positive aspects and in some cases the necessity of concentration by individuals on limited areas. And the chief standard by which to do this balancing, it seems to me, would be in terms of the degree to which a specialised mode of life isolates an individual from the community in which his specialism plays a part and the degree to which it degrades or elevates him in relation to the rest of the community, putting him in a position to be exploited or to exploit. The principle is thin; but it gains flesh by the reminder of the dangerous and often disastrous stupidity of 'experts' in our society, whose education and financing creates castes of ignorant and arrogant oracles with little ability to apply their abstract models to concrete reality or to bring their narrow skills to bear on wider problems. (Doctor-worshippers should read Ivan Illich's *Medical Nemesis,* Marion Boyars, (London, 1975) before they offer the ritual thanksgiving prayer to specialisation that usually occurs at this stage of the argument.) I have stressed the dangers of centralisation and linked the centralisation of power with the maintenance of hierarchical divisions. But 'centralisation' need not be the equivalent of 'oligarchy', since, in one sense it is compatible with the process of 'assembling' community policy and managing its execution in ways that are radically democratic. Since this conscious co-ordination would occur at any level of a democratic society, from abode upwards, it is a question not so much of whether or not to have 'centralisation', but rather of its form, scale, and focus (by which term I refer to specific concerns, for example water-supply, transport, agriculture, and so on). Again, I suggest, the 'principle' is as banal as it is formal: at what point do 'technical' gains, 'economies of scale' for example, offset political and economic loss, loss both in control and in richness of life? (At what point, in Mao's simile, does the lake get emptied to catch fish?) Again, however, discussion of such principles should not lose sight of the fact that we are discussing them from within a culture in which communal bonds and resources have been smashed and their role appropriated by the nation-state, and that we have difficulty seeing 'overall direction' emerging in any other form than state-commandism. And again we need to remind ourselves of the bungling destruction that has been carried on by monopolists and bureaucrats in the name of 'central planning' and in the interests of corporations responsible to no one but their shareholders. It is against this background that I am proposing the democratic control of production by those who do it and consume its fruits, and it is in this context that specialisation and centralisation as we have them today can be seen as mutually reinforcing obstacles.

The liberation of work feeds on itself, for the freer work becomes, the less is the need for authoritarian pressures to work. In this process bureaucrats and all sorts of ill-employed agents of capitalist life will have to move themselves off the backs and minds of the people and set about transforming themselves from policemen to producers. In all this it is not a question of 'levelling down' to some pre-given minimum, or of 'obliterating differences', but more of levelling 'up' and of replacing oppressive differences with community forms which respect individuality. At no time will that utopia when 'administration alone' replaces politics be on the cards; always there will be disagreements, struggles, and injustices. But to write and think as if the problems in envisioning a socialist democracy, problems all too superficially examined here, justify people in thinking of the status quo as either inevitable or desirable, in taking it for granted, is to whitewash the chaos and oppression of our social order.

FORENSIC PHILOSOPHY

The Discreet Violence of Bourgeois Law

To the untutored mind, it is in the law that the state's coercive power is most obvious. Yet the law is not presented as an instrument of power. Rather, like the Divine Law of which the Church supposedly serves as the mouthpiece, the law, or the abstraction 'Law', is represented as the guiding principle of the state itself. Thus the state, through legislation and especially through the daily judgments of judges, functions as the authoritative interpreter and enforcer of canons whose sources are far higher and far deeper than the contingencies of political power in the society:

> The moving spirit of the Constitution is to be found, then, in a certain characteristic of the English mind, which can best be described as attachment to law, as a sense that in the law and in law - they are not quite the same thing - there resides an authority superior to any power in the State: In the words of Bacon, 'The people of this Kingdom love the laws thereof, and nothing will oblige them more than an assurance of enjoying them; what the nobles once said upon occasion in Parliament, *nolumus leges Angliae mutari*, is imprinted in the hearts of all the people'. (Sir Maurice Amos, *The English Constitution,* London, 1930, p. 33)

The State then is not so much the imposer of rules as their materialisation, and the courts, police, prisons and prison officials are not there to hurt anyone, but to materialise 'society's moral code', to be, in Durkheim's words, 'a palpable symbol through which an inner state ('vigorous disapproval' of transgressors) is represented' *(Moral Education,* Free Press, 1961, p. 176).

The law court is a different world from that of ordinary life; it stands to daily affairs as church on Sundays stands to what

goes on in a working week. Its procedure is a moral melo-
drama, a repeatedly staged representation that, within its
walls at least, things are as they ought to be: given every
chance to establish that he is not guilty, the accused, once
found guilty, gets, at the command of a judicial patriarch,
what is coming to him - as it should be. Thus, according to the
story, he is punished, potential wrongdoers are deterred, and
respectable members of society can rest safer, content in the
knowledge that another who, unlike them, tried to flout
society's rules, has not got away with it but has had to pay the
price. In keeping with the court's solemn purpose, its cham-
ber and ritual connote a sublime majesty: His Honour's wigs
and robes set him apart, while his physical elevation, rein-
forced by the trappings of deference, place his judgment
above that of ordinary men. Prefaced by a sermon, a solemn
pronouncement of sentence sees the defendant taken from
the dock to receive his just deserts, while the 'mental attitude
which best becomes us', the law-abiding witnesses of this
moral ritual, '... is not pity but solemn exultation' (*Salmond on
Jurisprudence,* 11th ed. 1957 p.121). The official past of the
wrongdoer is the commission by him, of his own free will, of a
crime. His official future is 'punishment'. Behind this idealised
and abstract trajectory is a real past leading to the indicted
action, arrest and arraignment; and, stretching ahead, is a real
future, cut off from family and friends and consisting of
official and unofficial violence, a time of debilitating and
pointless isolation and tedium, a corrupting living death. But
such things are peripheral to the law's official mission as the
official guardian of official civil life. A hideous past becomes
'a disgraceful record' and a hideous future becomes a lesson.
Posturing as the uncontaminated arbiters of men and women's ways, the dispensers of legal violence need to be on a
pedestal separating out their activities from the illegal violence they are supposedly dealing with. They have to seem
aloof moreover, as the keystones of 'society', from the
political forces of which they are the products and protectors
—as Edmund Burke said: 'the magistrate must have his
reverence, the laws their authority'. The reverential vision of
law is not as widely shared as its priests would wish. But
certainly it is a vision encouraged among the students of law

themselves; those thousands who are to unite social duty and pecuniary interest by becoming the law's career-mediators. In the law-schools, the textbooks and courses detach law from its entrapment in human history, while 'Jurisprudence' purifies it into the distilled articulation of moral reasoning. And, in 'The Philosophy of Law', through H.L.A. Hart's *The Concept of Law,* (Oxford, 1961), the student discovers an *a priori* philosophy to do justice to the purity of his vocation. It is this philosophy and its sublimation of law and of the state of which it is the cutting edge, into the ideal form of 'rules' and 'obligations' that will now be examined.

Legitimation Through Sublimation: Hart's *Concept of Law*
Hart's book, which remains the standard text in its field, sets out to supplant the doctrine of Hobbes, Bentham and Austin *(The Province of Jurisprudence Determined,* 1832). According to this 'classical positivist' view, laws are commands backed by threats, issued to subjects by their 'sovereign'. The sovereign, whether individual monarch or institution, is not, *qua* sovereign, itself subject to law. Were it so subject, a higher authority would have to have jurisdiction over it and an infinite regress would be in store; and it is only a play on words to say that the sovereign is 'subject' to its own laws, since any rules 'followed' by the sovereign are voluntarily followed, as evidenced by the sovereign's power to change laws that don't suit it. For a law to exist is for there to be a capacity and disposition on the part of a power to impose sanctions against disobedience of its commands, and for these sanctions to be effective, that is, for there to be a 'general disposition of obedience' on the part of the subjects. *De facto* power through the capacity to use force is thus the basis of the legal order. Thus this view denies any jurisprudential aloofness of law from the politics of the state. That-which-is-enforced is the law and, should I excuse my illegal conduct by denying that the commandment I have enfringed deserves to be called 'law', '... the court of justice will demonstrate the inconclusiveness of my reasoning by hanging me up'. Austin was a utilitarian, not an ethical relativist, and he recognised with more ease than Hobbes that a law could be vicious. But he looked to politics as the

sanction against abuse of power by the sovereign, for injustice might 'excite the anger and rouse to active resistance the
might which slumbers in the multitude' - Austin's sovereign is
not the only force in society and law therefore does reflect the
impact of subjects' *resistance*. A true theory of law would,
however, question Austin's tendency to conflate official
authority and power and would specifically reject his identification of the official sovereign accepted by the courts ('The
Queen in Parliament', say,) with the dominant power in the
land. An adequate theory would also question Austin's
failure to look at legalism as an ideological force reinforcing
relations in capitalist society, with its individual 'rights and
duties' and its whole ideology of individual responsibility.
But, especially as its refusal to prettify is itself an encourage-
ment to realism, Austinian positivism could be a basis for
theory in this field. *The Province of Jurisprudence Determined*, however, has been unread for several decades and
Austin is used in our law schools largely as a foil for Hart.

It is Hart's aim to establish a decent mental interval
between his own view and the Hobbes-Bentham-Austin
'commands-backed-by-threats' perspective. The command
model, which Hart characterises as the 'top-to-bottom' model, pictures the legal order as, in his phrase, 'The Gunman
Situation Writ Large', the holdup-man being the clearest
case of someone issuing orders backed by force. Hart then
sets out to show the distance between the law and this
paradigm. Let us examine Hart's contrasts.

(i) *Laws as Standards of Conduct: 'Laws have a Normative Function'*

The command theory operates with the concepts 'order',
'threat', 'capacity to enforce', 'compliance'. But, says Hart,
laws are rules, and:

> ... where rules exist, deviations from them are not merely
> grounds for a prediction that hostile reactions will follow or
> that a court will apply sanctions to those who break them, but
> they are also a *reason* or *justification* for applying sanctions.
> (*Concept of Law*, p. 82)

This, says Hart is the 'fundamental objection' to the brute order-threat view.

Hart writes of laws as 'standards for the guidance of society', as if the guidance provided were of an essentially moral kind and as if breach of such 'standards', in itself, justified the imposition of sanctions. Threats of force are said to be 'secondary', so there is no question of the 'guidance' being guidance in avoiding trouble from the police; 'law is equally if not more concerned with the 'puzzled' man or the 'ignorant' man who is willing to do what is required if only he can be told what it is' (p. 39). Hart emphasises the 'moral' vocabulary of law - 'ought', 'obligation', 'norm', 'duty', 'justification' - as against the coercive vocabulary that is central to the Austinian framework. Moreover, in accordance with then current Oxford practice, he frequently likens laws to rules of games, as if laws constituted social life's contests in the way that rules constitute games; a sporting view of things, certainly.

Hart says, incontrovertibly, that to embrace the law as a standard of conduct is to have the 'internal point of view' and he criticises theorists who ignore this 'essential' aspect by treating laws as mere threats. Now it is not clear to me that Austin, who, as a utilitarian, regarded this kind of rule-worship as a superstition, would have been unable to recognise its existence: to recognise, that is, the role of 'internalised sanctions' in society; Hume, Bentham and Paley, after all, went to some lengths to show the importance of conditioned fears in keeping society 'in order'. Certainly Hart is right to stress, however confusedly, the ideological aspect of law. Legalistic modes of thinking and of seeing things tend to pervade our social lives and institutions, and it is a measure of a legal system's security of power that it can get away with presenting its conduct as on 'society's' behalf. But this ideological penetration should itself be the object of critical questioning in legal theory; it is no part of that theory to treat such ideologies as a given basis of analysis. An adequate theory of law, moreover, would need to take account of the countervailing tendency of official conduct to tailor itself to prevailing norms and ideologies, sometimes of an 'anti-legalistic' kind, and would need to trace the delicate circumspection that is required for the maintenance of 'credibility' (Douglas Hay's 'Property, Authority and Criminal Law' in Hay, Thompson *et al*: *Albion's Fatal Tree,* Allen Lane, 1975, treats this and other questions pertinent to developing a realistic materialist alternative to Hart's legal formalism). But, in any case, from the point of view of assessing Hart's own view, it does not much matter, for it emerges that the 'internal point of view', the ignoring of which was Austin's 'fundamental defect', need after all be held only by 'the officials or experts of the system' (pp. 60, 113), so that what had earlier been erected as moral signposts for society become nothing more than the procedural rules accepted and followed by professional legislators and executives of the system: the 'internal' point of view, by definition, is the point of view of those on the inside, while:

> The ordinary citizen manifests his acceptance largely by acquiescence in the results of ... official operations. He keeps the law which is made and identified in this way, and also makes claims and exercises powers conferred by it. But he may know little of its origins or of its makers: some may know nothing more of the laws than that they are 'the Law'. It forbids things ordinary citizens want to do and they know that they might be arrested by a policeman and sent to prison by a judge if they disobey. (p. 60)

Again:

> So long as the laws which are valid by the system's tests of validity are obeyed by the bulk of the population this is surely all the evidence we need in order to establish that a given legal system exists. (p. 111)

So where are we? Once the moralistic veneer of Hart's talk about the Internal and the External has been peeled away, we are back to the very substance he had claimed to reject. We are left with the command theory, supplemented by the truism that legal officials and lawyers 'effectively accept' (p. 113) the rules in terms of which they carry on their professional lives. Outside the august bureaus of the legal establishment, whose own rules may be presumed to be valid to itself, the masses are down even more surely where they were left by Austin's sovereign: at the bottom. And so Hart's 'fundamental objection' to the command theory of law emerges as little more than a quibble.

Hart's basic intentions tear each other apart. He wants to get away from the Austinian focus on the coercive power of the state by stressing the 'moral' force of the legal 'ought'; on the other hand, in contrast with the natural law theorists, such as Lon Fuller *(The Morality of Law,* Yale, 1964), he wants to identify law, not with substantial moral practices, with just procedures, but with the *de facto* practices of bodies of 'officials and experts'. Thus he oscillates between moralism and positivism, succeeding only in presenting blurred apologetics for the legal bureaucracy and dissolving their power into mere forms. It is as if one were to notice of a ballroom seducer only that he dances in time. Hart writes as if the Hobbes-Bentham-Austin tradition has place only for brute force and is therefore blind to the cultural and ideological context of law. But this context, and its attendant constraints have been recognised even in the most Hobbesian circles. William Paley, of that ilk, articulated the difficulty well:

> ... even in the least popular forms of civil government, the physical strength lies in the governed. In what manner opinion thus prevails over strength, or how power is maintained in opposition to it; in other words, by what motives the many are induced to submit to the few, becomes an inquiry which lies at the root of almost every political speculation ...; let them be admonished ... that general opinion therefore ought always to be treated with deference, and managed with delicacy and circumspection. *Principles of Moral and Political Philosophy,* 1785, Book VI, Chapter 2)

(ii) *Law as Self-restraint: 'Legislation, as distinct from just ordering others to do things under threats, may perfectly well have a self-binding force' (p. 42)*

The gunman pushes others around. But, says Hart, legislators typically are themselves bound, as indeed everyone in the territory is, by the laws they pass. James Callaghan, Margaret Thatcher, are themselves subject to the laws passed by 'the Queen in Parliament'. So impressed is Hart by the constitutional humility of legislators and their 'self-binding' that he thinks that the activity of promising' '... is in many ways a far better model than that of coercive orders for understanding many though not all features of law' (p. 42).

Now it might be asked whether constitutional rule is essential to law; have not rulers proclaimed themselves above the law without thereby denying that they rule through law? In any case, 'self-binding' was fully recognised in Austin's system, which distinguished the institutional capacity of legislators, *qua* sovereign, from their capacity as 'ordinary citizens', ordinary citizens, we might note in connection with Richard Nixon and associates, whose capacity to remove themselves from the ties with which they have bound themselves is the envy of other ordinary citizens. Hart notes the universality of laws - they bind every one - and thus stresses the inherent justice of law. I do not deny that 'the rule of law' in this sense is important, or that it cannot be contrasted with purely arbitrary tyranny. (This is provocatively discussed in the final chapter of E.P. Thompson's *Whigs and Hunters,* Allen Lane, 1976.) But formal self-regulation is compatible with substantial partiality and other - domination with, that is, the substantial truth of the top-to-bottom' view. Anatole France observed that the law in its majesty equally forbids both rich and poor to sleep under bridges; we might note that it is equally binding on the agents and sufferers of a system not to disturb the system.

In any case, realism would require that we examine the degree to which different sections of the establishment do in practice work within the bounds of law, and the extent to which, For Reasons of State, they break or go over the law 'in order to keep it'. William Colby, of the C.I.A. (who ought to know) says, 'there is a law in every country that says no, and almost every country does it'. Police and prison guards operate, to greater or lesser degrees, as 'laws unto themselves', and judges have such a degree of discretion in the way they treat cases that they 'make law' while pretending to merely follow it. On the basis of his study of judicial conduct in eighteenth-century England, Douglas Hay has this to say of court-formalism:

> The punctilious attention to forms, the dispassionate and legalistic exchanges between counsel and the judge, argued

that those administering and using the laws submitted to its rules. The law thereby became something more than the creature of a ruling class—it became a power with its own claims, higher than those of prosecutor, lawyers, and even the scarlet-robed assize judge himself. To them, too, of course, the law was The Law. The fact that they reified it, that they shut their eyes to its daily enactment in Parliament by men of their own class, heightened the illusion. When the ruling class acquitted men on technicalities they helped instil a belief in the disembodied justice of the law in the minds of those who watched. In short, its very inefficiency, its absurd formalism, was part of its strength as ideology. (*'Property, Authority and the Criminal Law', (Albion's Fatal Tree, p.33)*)

(iii) Laws as Enablers: 'There are important classes of law where this analogy with orders backed by threats altogether fails, since they perform a quite different social function. Legal rules defining the ways in which valid contracts or wills or marriages are made do not require persons to act in certain ways whether they wish to or not. Such laws do not impose duties or obligations. Instead they provide individuals with facilities for realizing their wishes, by conferring legal powers upon them to create, by certain specified procedures, subject to certain conditions, structures of rights and duties within the coercive framework of law'. (p. 27)

Hart names such rules 'power-conferring rules'. Contract and inheritance, then, are capacities, 'contributions to social life' (p. 28) constituting the civil law. Whereas the criminal law does impose restrictions, the civil law directly widens the scope of individual choice and agency. Now certainly there is a difference between 'don't steal!' and 'if you want a television set you have to pay such and such an amount': the former appears 'negative', 'categorical', while the latter appears 'positive', 'hypothetical', telling you how to go about getting what you want - if you happen to want it.

But, remembering that 'possession is nine-tenths of the law' and that criminal laws against property transgression and civil laws which specify what counts as valid ownership must be mutually implicated, we might well suspect Hart's neat dichotomy of 'obligation-imposing' and 'power-conferring' laws. Laws specifying propriety of ownership and

laws banning appropriation by other means, are mutually
implicated dimensions of the same system-maintaining
activity - if you want a television, you have to go about it this
way, you cannot go about it that way. And so, is there, after
all, such a gulf between the implications of 'if you want a
television set you have to pay such and such an amount' and
'if you want to avoid fines or imprisonment, pay such and
such an amount for your television set'? In the Austinian
tradition it is said that civil laws have sanctions, just as
criminal laws do: specifically, civil laws have a 'sanction of
nullity' just as prison is a criminal sanction. Thus, for
example, non-payment has as its painful consequence the
fact that the television deal is off, the attempted purchase is
nullified. Hart objects that, whereas nullity is the tautological consequence of failure to follow the correct civil
procedure, the 'sanctions proper' associated with the criminal law are logically detachable from the offence (p. 34)
—the person who steals is not necessarily punished. But
this point depends solely on the choice of description. That
breaches of criminal law are, *qua* breach, 'to be punished' is
tautological. On the other hand, the substantial 'sanction of
nullity' suffered by the person who has failed to pay is not the
trivial consequence that he has failed to make a *proper*
purchase, it is that he lacks a television set, just as eviction is
the substantial sanction associated with the 'nullity' of a rent
transaction. And such commonly conferred forms of powerlessness are clearly logically detachable from the legal
"nullity" of the act - just as the police may not arrest the
criminal, you might get a television set without the proper
procedure. Generally, the law's laying down what you can do
as well as what you cannot do are two sides of the same coin,
whose 'contribution to social life' cannot be read of *a priori*.

Hart writes as if the private property system exists as a
legally bestowed instrument of human welfare. But the law's
historical role has been as much to reinforce emerging
property forms and hence class forms, as to create them.
Even today business contracts are made in ways to which the
law is secondary, credit functioning as a sanction, while the
law is typically brought into the situation only where it is
thought necessary to use special force to impose interests.

More important, Hart legalistically ignores the substantially coercive nature of property as we have it (or lack it): to characterise a labour-contract as essentially a 'facility' whereby a worker gets to be able to work or gets to be able to feed his family, while the "other party" gets to augment his profit is, as argued earlier, to mock real life. Private property means control, power over-and-against other individuals. A will is individious: it excludes as it bestows. Deprivation of goods is as much a sanction of the property system is imprisonment; you cannot read off the social thrust of laws from the verbal formulae they are couched in, or from the section of the textbooks they are catalogued in - once again Bentham and Austin, who defended the property system on substantial grounds, espoused a more coherent position than Hart. (See Bentham on 'The Levelling System', *Works'* Vol. 1, p. 385.) Different courts operate in different atmospheres - from John Doe the respected businessman fined £30 for misrepresenting his product on the market, to the 'vicious type' given years for picketing, so one would not be wrong in noting that whereas the courts seem concerned to 'facilitate' some kinds of activities, they are equally concerned to 'de-facilitate' activities disruptive or subversive of the former. But the contrast between a reprimand for crime in the suites and imprisonment for crime in the streets hardly overturns the top-to-bottom view of law. It reminds us, rather, who is on top, and suggests another resonance for the notion of 'the internal standpoint':

> The financial details of the marriage settlement, so often the sacrament by which land allied itself with trade, provided the best lawyers with a good part of their fees. But if most of the law and the lawyers were concerned with the civil dealings which propertied men had with one another, most men, the unpropertied labouring poor, met the law as criminal sanction: the threat or the reality of whipping, transportation, and hanging. ('Property, Authority and the Criminal Law', *Albion's Fatal Tree, p. 22)*

Hart uses his category of 'power-conferring rules', not only as a counter-example to the command theory, but as a model for his own general view of law as 'the union of primary and secondary rules'. We shall see that the use of this model leaves Hart with a picture of law at least as awesome as those he tries to replace.

(iv) Rules as Power-makers: 'Rules are constitutive of the sovereign, not merely things we should have to mention in a description of habits of obedience to the sovereign' (p. 75)

Austin claimed that the 'sovereign' could not be legally bound. Hart claims that rules, 'secondary rules', themselves specify the sovereign, so that he espouses a kind of *a priori* constitutionalism. In developing his view and to bring out its logical structure, Hart makes use of an historical model, a model of the transition of society from the pre-legal to the legal condition. We shall examine this at some length.

The Law as white man's magic

Hart asks us to consider a primitive community, devoid of courts, legislature, officials of any kind. Its conduct is, we are told, controlled by 'the general attitude of the group towards its own standard modes of behaviour' (p. 89). Now, says Hart, if social life is to go on at all, given its universal temptations, there will have to be rules, and especially rules forbidding violence, theft, and deception. Such are 'primary rules', imposing obligations. It emerges that this primitive society suffers from severe 'defects', particularly 'uncertainty', 'stasis', and 'inefficiency'. It also emerges that the cure for these defects is the white man's medicine: Law. Let us, (with Hart), diagnose these defects.

Uncertainty: In the primitive situation, doubts about the rules cannot be settled 'either by reference to an authoritative text or to an official whose declaration on this point is authoritative' (p. 90).

Stasis: 'There will be no means in such a society for deliberately adapting the rules to changing circumstances either by eliminating old rules or introducing new ones' (p. 90).

Inefficiency: In the absence of 'special agencies' to determine that a breach has occurred and to capture and punish, there will be, among other miseries, 'a waste of time in the group's unorganized efforts to catch and punish offenders' (p. 91).

What solves these shortcomings of primitive societies?
They dissolve with the supplementation of primary rules by
secondary rules, which

> ...specify the ways in which the primary rules may be con-
> clusively ascertained, introducted, eliminated, varied, and the
> fact of their violation conclusively determined. (p. 92)

What is needed, then, are 'power-conferring rules' estab-
lishing a network of legislators, judges and police, a network
whose 'internal point of view' we have already seen to be
central to Hart's analysis. Let us observe this transforming
witchcraft.

Uncertainty will be relieved, Hart says, if laws are presented, perhaps 'carved on some public monument' (p. 92),
and especially if a 'rule of recognition' 'is introduced' according to which the only rules to be regarded as binding are rules
'enacted by a specific body'. Stasis is abolished at the same
stroke: a 'rule of change' 'is introduced' 'which empowers an
individual or body of persons to introduce new primary rules'
(p. 93), while the 'introduction' of a judiciary and a police
force put an end to inefficiency.

So unruliness is ended: by rules. But since, *ex hypothesi*,
there is trouble among the natives, there will no doubt be
rivals who, with convenient literacy, will inscribe these
convenient monuments with rival 'laws'. Hart, oblivious to
the centrality of political power, simply ignores this awkward
possibility. Suppose rival forces promulgate rival claims to
recognition. Must new rules be 'introduced' - by whom? - to
resolve this higher uncertainty? How, we might wonder, did
these 'static' natives, unable, in the absence of professional
specialists, to 'deliberately adapt', deliberately bring in this
new rule of change making change possible? Did it need a
prior rule of change, shouted from the heavens or from a
British jeep, to make that rule's introduction possible? And
who in all this colonialistic and paternalistic myth is supposed
to be recognizing and empowering whom? Hart, with the
idealism characteristic of legalistic thought, seems to regard
rules and officials as magical forces sufficiently powerful
themselves to drive away native superstition; as remedies
untouched by the ills they are sent to cure—

> usually some official certificate or official copy will, under the
> rules of recognition, be taken as sufficient proof of due
> enactment. (p. 93)

It is as if there were authorities in this orgy of self-
certification, whose function is to 'introduce' authority.
'Self-help', says Hart is 'inefficient' - a judiciary and a
police force come in, therefore, to cure this disorder of social
infantilism. But the institution of a special administrative
apparatus breaks down the networks of self-administration,
and in the name of 'efficiency' creates a body of non-
productive people, needing to be fed, clothed, and housed,
who constitute an élitist and repressive force in the society.
The ends and interests whose 'efficient' service is supposedly guaranteed by all this are never specified - who
then, determines that they are 'doing their job'? Themselves,
or some other specialised body?

Hart proposes 'rules of recogniton' as constituting the cure
of primitive ills. But the idea of the primitive society as being
without 'rules of recognition', in the only sense in which any
society has them, is incoherent. Despite its absence of official
certificates, a society without specialised officials is not
necessarily a society without 'recognised' authorities. What
is specific to such a society is that everyone who 'knows the
way' is an authority, and that this knowledge is distributed
throughout the society - look at who listens to whom, and you
have the 'rules' of recognition. This connects with Hart's
ignoring of the evolution of law in the struggles for power
consequent on the breakdown of primitive cohesion. He
writes, in fact, as if 'the authorities', recognisable, con-
spicuous, were ready to move in with their constitution-filled
briefcases. Now, in a manner of speaking, this may well be
close to the case in the colonial and neo-colonial situation
with which the British are familiar; but such situations are
paradigmatic of situations where 'duly recognised authority'
rides desperately on the back of duly exercised coercive
power. Yet it is power, the key to Austin's understanding of
law, that Hart's analysis is geared to conceal. Consider,
however, what it is, according to Hart's considered judgement, for a certain 'rule of recognition' to exist. Hart tells us

on pages 98, 107, and 108 that it amounts to no more than an 'actual practice' on the part of officials of following certain procedures and accepting certain sources of authority for their official actions. And so the very existence of these rules, which is supposed to underlie the system, in fact presupposes a certain structure of power - to say that a certain rule of recognition exists is not to say much more than that someone is in power. So, through the idealist formulations, we are not very far from Austin's materialism. The idea of sovereignty as 'rule-governed' collapses into the idea that a certain institutionalised source of law is 'effectively accepted' by courts, police and other specialised and often self-certificated bodies. And this collapse is a reminder of the fragility of Hart's use of 'power-conferring rules' as his model for the 'secondary rules' constituting legal authority. Certainly Hart's 'rules of recognition' 'facilitate' the activities of what-ever legal bureaucracy may invoke them; but it emerges that this facilitation is boundless; this constitutionalism therefore vacuous. But the power to make a contract, Hart's original model for state and court power, is legally restricted—you cannot validly contract to commit a crime. Hence the very model chosen by Hart functions to reinforce the idealist illusion of rule-boundedness, whereas no state crimes are rules out by the 'rules of recognition'; all we have are the verbal trappings of official propriety. From a different pers-pective, Stanley Diamond, an anthropologist who shares neither Hart's disdain for facts nor his contempt for non-English culture, analyses the development of law in the context of the development of the state, itself understood in terms of the struggle of elites to establish themselves as a ruling class through a 'cannibalistic' onslaught on preexisting community relations:

> As the integrity of local groups declined, a process which, in the autochthonous state, must have taken generations or even centuries, conditions doubtless developed which served as an *ex post facto* rationalization for edicts already in effect. In this sense, laws become self-fulfilling prophecies. Crime and the laws which served it were, then, co-variants of the evolving state system. ('The Rule of Law and the Order of Custom', in R.P. Wolff ed., *The Rule of Law*, New York, 1971, p. 132)

Thus Hart's variant of 'the social contract' fails to establish its general claims. And in the course of his argument, as we have seen, he casually exhibits the legal chauvinism so characteristic of the disastrous constitution-mongers of British colonialism. Against this kind of talk, S.F. Nadel discusses the significance of 'law' among the Nupe of Nigeria and notes:

> ...a much more subtle development and a deeper kind of antagonism (than that between states), namely, the almost eternal antagonism of developed state versus that raw material of the community which, always and everywhere, must form the nourishing soil from which alone the state can grow.

Moreover:

> What did the tax-paying, law-abiding citizen receive in return for allegiance to king and nobility? Was extortion bribery, brutal force, the only aspect under which the state revealed itself to the populace? The people were to receive ... one thing: security - protection against external and internal enemies, and general security for carrying out daily work, holding markets, using the roads ... We have seen what security and protection meant in reality. At their very best, they represented something very unequal and very unstable. The situation must have led to much tension and change within the system and to frequent attempts to procure better safeguards for civil rights. ('Nupe State and Community', *Africa*, Volume 8, pp. 303, 287)

Western legal institutions, forms and philosophies have been vigorously exported to the third world as part of the neo-colonial bequest, and Hart's book is part of that bequest. Summarising his paper 'Law and Cultural Colonialism: Questioning some Assumptions about Law and Development', John Goldring writes:

> Many lawyers from the former metropolitan powers ... are in fact furthering the economic domination by the rich countries of the poor 'developing' countries and increasing the gap between rich and poor nations. Colonial legal systems and 'modern' legal systems which have been imposed on developing countries are inappropriate. They may not only crush indigenous traditions, but may in fact be the cause of social disharmony within the developing countries. The emergence of legal professionals in the developing countries may be/a

political force acting against the interests of the developing nations and for social divisions. (University of Sydney Faculty of Law, 1974)

Natural Law; or the Prudent Despot

Hart is a formalist and he rejects (in Chapter 9 especially) the 'natural law' theorists' claim that law properly-so-called must have a certain content, must, that is, embody principles of justice. Law, for Hart, is law in virtue of its official accreditation, not in virtue of its just edicts. Nonetheless, he does argue that if a 'social organisation' is to be 'viable', it must maintain 'certain rules of conduct' (p. 188). And so given general conditions under which people are governable, it is necessary that law should have a minimum content, which Hart is prepared to call 'the minimum content of natural law'.

> In the absence of this content, men, as they are, would have no reason for obeying voluntarily any rules; and without a minimum of co-operation given voluntarily by those who find it is in their interest to submit to and maintain the rules, coercion of others who do not voluntarily conform would be impossible. (p. 189)

Such is the 'general form' of what amounts to a claim about the transcendental conditions of the possibility of a social order. 'The union of primary and secondary rules', it can now be seen, connotes the legislative content necessary to maintain the legislative form, by removing the motive to rebel from sufficient members of the population. How is this achieved? By taking into account basic 'truisms concerning human nature and the world in which men live'. Which truisms? That 'men' are vulnerable, approximately equal, of limited altruism, resources, and understanding. Hence to maintain a viable order, there must be laws which protect against violence, theft and exploitation, lest the motivation to obey disappear (shades of Harold Wilson's 'social contract') and the social organisation cease to be viable (p. 190-4).

Just how 'minimal' this safeguard is, Hart himself implicitly acknowledges within two pages, in a remark which abandons much of the ground that the book had appeared, however shakily, to occupy. With special reference to slavery and racism (viable enough), Hart observes of the law, now suddenly seen as an instrument of state:

> ...it may be used to subdue and maintain, in a position of permanent inferiority, a subject group whose size, relative to the master group, may be large or small, depending on the means of coercion, solidarity and discipline available to the latter, and the helplessness or inability to organise of the former. (p. 196)

Unfortunately, this belated critical recognition of law as an aspect of politics comes too late to shape the overall trajectory of Hart's overwhelmingly power-concealing book. Like a self-critical after-thought, it is tucked away, forgotten.

Consider the gunman situation writ moderately large: consider gang rule in a city. Within the gang and its supporters there are 'rules of recognition', accepted chains of command and accepted rules of succession. The gang may last many years and establish firm control over its territory or sphere of business. Under its rule life may be quite 'orderly' as those who pay up their protection-money are indeed protected and 'empowered' to make certain transactions. Far be it from me to liken the rulers of any modern, legally sophisticated societies to such a gang... But when official spectacles are removed, it is difficult to see important respects in which gang-rule fails to fulfil Hart's criteria for a legal system.

Hart's legalism, his 'apolitical' absorption in officialdom and its forms vitiates his account of what law is and what place it has in social life, turning what sets out as a humanistic critique of positivism into an idealistic apology for the *status quo*. Moreover, by erecting his faith in officials and experts into a full-blown social philosophy, Hart rules out of consideration the possibility that society might be organised along radically different lines, lines according to which 'people's law' might be, not the mockery that it is in Stalinese, but a living institutional form of popular self-government.

But even to discuss such a possibility requires that we look at law not 'abstractly', but in its complex place in the whole fabric of social life. It is the unfortunate tendency of Hart's standard text to reinforce the professional isolation of lawy-

ers by giving that isolation a conceptual underpinning. I hope
so far to have done something to show this underpinning's
inadequacy.

'Philosophy of Punishment': The Soft Sell of the Hard Cell

We have seen the degree to which Hart reflects and reinforces the tendency of legalism to bury social reality in a file
of red-taped patter. Nowhere is this burial more thorough
than in 'the philosophy of punishment', an allied field of
inquiry which appears to have as its overall aim the discovery
of 'a morally acceptable account' of the established judicial
and prison procedures and practices: 'the justification of
punishment'. From the time when St. Augustine discovered
theological reasons for killing infidels to the time when B.F.
Skinner discovered scientific reasons for treating criminals
like experimental pigeons, the practices which can be
brought under the label 'punishment' have been surrounded
with the utmost in pious circumspection and euphemism.
And our philosophers have obediently, even eagerly, bowed
their heads, closed their eyes, and joined in the chorus of
praise for that institution by whose grace we can sleep
unmolested in our beds at night. At the beginning of this
chapter I mentioned that the convicted criminal disappears
from the eyes of the law, as surely as from the public eye, with
the act of conviction and sentencing: he has been convicted;
his life *as convict* is of no public interest—having lost his
rights, afterall, he is no longer a member of the public
proper. It is enough that, according to emphasis, he is
undergoing 'punishment', 'learning his lesson', 'being re-
habilitated', 'copping it', 'put safely away'. Similarly for the
philosophers: obeying an unwritten rule not to think about
what actually goes on under whatever banners they wish to
champion ('utilitarian', 'retributive'), they adhere strictly to
the practice of referring to penal activities only under legitimating descriptions. Yet they assume *a priori* that what they
are justifying is indeed 'our practice', 'what we do'. (The
matter, as the bureaucrats say, is being taken care of.) Now
what happens when people are 'punished' is nothing other
than what happens when people are put, for example, in
prison. But if you look for a discussion of imprisonment in

our academic philosophers' works you won't find it; you won't even find the term in the index. And this is a symptom of the fact that what you are getting is not a conceptual investigation of reality but an investigation of concepts, whose relation to reality is not supposed to be a topic of polite conversation.

Traditionally punishment-philosophy has split into the camps of Retributivism, according to which punishment is justified by its being deserved, and Utilitarianism, according to which punishment is justified by its beneficial consequences on the individual and on the rest of society. Kant (see pp. 99-106 of *The Metaphysical Elements of Justice,* translated J. Ladd, Bobbs-Merrill, 1965) presents classical retributivism, and Bentham (see *Principles of Penal Law* in *Works* edited by Bowring, Volume 1) presents utilitarianism in its classic form. I shall discuss Bentham and Kant's affinities later. But recent philosophers, Hart prominent among them, have claimed to crack this antinomy by separating out different questions to which the two, apparently rival, theories are answers. Utilitarianism, thus properly understood, addresses itself to the question of the 'General Justifying Aim' of punishment - answer: the protection of society, while retributivism, shorn of its 'freewill' metaphysics, is the answer to the question who should be punished - answer: those guilty of breaking society's rules. Now, while agreeing with Ted Honderich (*Punishment*, Penguin 1970) that the attempt thus to create a sort of dualism between the justification of a practice in general and the justification of a particular instance of such a practice is sophistical (see Honderich, especially p. 151 and following), what I want to draw attention to is the way such a division fosters the conservative rationalisation of which I am concerned to convict my learned colleagues. For, if one concentrates only on the 'arguments', what is missed is the curious fact that the debaters all seem to agree on one thing: that, whatever its justification, what we have is more or less justifiable.

Punishment as Debt Collection: Bourgeois Punology

Hart's view is roughly this: by 'announcing standards of behaviour' the law establishes networks of reciprocal rights and duties. Its coercive machinery protects those networks, hence 'society' 'attaches penalties' to forms of conduct that, by breaching reciprocities, are 'harmful'. But, by announcing these penalties in advance, the law gives individuals 'the option between obeying or paying', and hence punishment 'appears as a price justly extracted because the criminal had a fair opportunity beforehand to avoid liability to pay' ('Prolegomenon to the Principles of Punishment' in *Punishment and Responsibility*, Oxford, 1968, pp. 22-3). So, despite gestures of doubt, Hart leaves unshaken the idea that the law does indeed protect a society characterised by reciprocity, by justice. Given that, it is easy to take it that the person who knowingly and voluntarily (not in a fit, etc., etc.) breaks the law can be said to be acting in a peculiarly harmful and exploitative way, and, moreover, since all are assumed to be well protected, to have done so freely and without constraint —gratuitously as it were. Thus is postulated an idealized background which can be left implicit when, convicted, he is sentenced to 'pay his price'.

The 'two questions' to which utilitarianism and retributivism are supposed to be the distinct answers are, in fact not so separate: rather it is against the background of an idealised 'answer' to the 'first question', (that of the law's 'general function'), that the attention is focused on the 'second', (is he 'guilty'?) as if it were solely in virtue of having broken the law that the culprit's comeuppance was justified. (Anyone who has participated in examiners meetings or disciplinary proceedings at a university will be familiar with this blinkering process.)

Herbert Morris, in an article 'Persons and Punishment' (reprinted in a collection *Punishment and Rehabilitation*, edited by J.G. Murphy, Wadsworth, California, 1973), follows Hart in articulating a utilitarian retributivism and, often using Hart's own locutions, brings out even more clearly the aspect of the bourgeois ideology of punishment that I am talking about.

> Applying to the conduct of men are a group of rules, ones I shall label 'primary', which closely resemble the core rules of our criminal law... compliance with which provides benefits for all persons... Making possible this mutual benefit is the assumption by individuals of a burden. The burden consists in

the excercise of self-restraint by individuals over inclinations
that would, if satisfied, directly interfere... with others in
proscribed ways. If a person fails to exercise self-restraint... he
renounces a burden which others have assumed and thus gains
an advantage... A person who violates the rules has something
others have—the benefits of the system—but by renouncing
what others have assumed, the burdens of self-restraint, he has
acquired an unfair advantage. Matters are not even until this
advantage is in some way erased. Another way of putting it is
that he owes something to others... Justice—that is, punishing
such individuals - restores the equilibrium of burdens by taking
from the individual what he owes, that is, exacting the debt.
(pp. 42-3)

Like Hart, Morris is intoxicated by formal equalities and
reciprocities (his only criticism of existing penal systems are
formal ones). He simply assumes both that 'all persons'
benefit from such rules and that the law is in fact concerned to
penalise equally all breaches of them. We live, it would seem,
in a market which, but for those who break its rules, would be
perfect. Hence the law's function is to restore the market's
equilibrium by exacting the price from those who have sought
to avoid payment. The long arm of the law thus supplements
the invisible hand of the bourgeois economy. Kropotkin had
a firmer grasp of reality:

> To begin with, there is the fact that none of the prisoners
> recognise the justice of the punishment inflicted on them. This
> is in itself a condemnation of our whole judicial system... How
> many times have you heard prisoners say: 'It's the big thieves
> who are holding us here; we are the little ones'. Who can
> dispute this when he knows the incredible swindles perpetrated
> in the realm of high finance and commerce; when he knows
> that the thirst for riches, acquired by every possible means, is
> the very essence of bourgeois society... gaols are made for the
> unskilful, not for criminals... Whether in regard to food or the
> distribution of favours, in the words of the prisoners from San
> Fransisco to Kamtchatka: 'The biggest thieves are those who
> hold us here, not ourselves'. *Revolutionary Pamphlets*, edited
> by R.N. Baldwin, Dover 1970, pp. 222-3)

In a world of sanctioned exploitation it is grotesque to treat
criminal sanctions as society's protection against exploit-

ation. In a world of official vandalism, thuggery, blackmail, corruption and murder it is hypocrisy to talk as if law were the means whereby officials protect us 'self-restrainers' from these things. In a world in which invidious dominance and invidious possessions are held out as the height of aspiration it is a mockery to speak as if those to whom illegal violence and theft appear as the means of attaining these goals have the privilege of an unconstrained choice to obey or disobey the laws, to pretend that the 'exploiters' whose punishment 'restores the equilibrium of benefits and burdens' do not come in fact overwhelmingly from the most burdened and exploited section of the population, so that imprisonment and police harassment, far from presenting equilibrium, rather doubles the punishments of class privation. Kropotkin again:

> What does the child growing up in the streets see? Luxury, stupid and insensate, smart shops, reading matter devoted to exhibiting wealth, a money-worshipping cult developing a thirst for riches, a passion for living at the expense of others. The catchword is 'Get rich. Destroy everything that stands in your way, and do it by any means save those that will land you in goal'. Manual labour is despised to a point where the ruling classes prefer to indulge in gymnastics rather than handle a spade or saw. A calloused hand is considered a sign of inferiority and a silk dress of superiority.
>
> Society itself daily creates these people incapable of leading a life of honest labour, and filled with anti-social desires. She glorifies them when their crimes are crowned by financial success. She sends them to prison when they have not 'succeeded'. (*Pamphlets*, p. 232)

We live in criminal and criminogenic societies in which many of the activities of enforcement agencies are taken up with activities merely stigmatized as 'crime', with the ritual maintenance of respectability.

Not only is the law a relatively weak instrument for combating this dominant tendency of our society, its own dominant tendency is to safeguard that society's dominant, that is capitalist, practices. But, if we refuse to follow legalism into its mazes of abstraction, we can see, as few punitivists since Bentham have done, that the 'punishment' that concerns 'the philosophers of punishment', namely that connected with the criminal law, is but the bottom in a disciplinary hierarchy of penalties. If pauperism is the sanction against the refusal to labour for a wage, imprisonment is the sanction against attempts to avoid pauperism without wage-labour. Thus does criminal punishment have to be seen in the terms of politico-economic processes by which 'life-chances', 'rewards and punishments', are imposed in a society. But, by the same token in emphasising the common characteristics of eviction, the sack, a smack, being kept in after school, losing pay, being fined, and being imprisoned, and in emphasising the many forms of 'policing' by which order is maintained, it is essential also to examine the specific nature and function of different types of 'punishment', (exile, branding, stocks, whipping, fining, hanging, torture, etc., etc.) and to take seriously for example, the remarkable fact that very few people in prisons actually regard what is being done to them as 'punishment' at all.

So what we are offered in the way of 'utilitarian' justifications of punishment is typically an *a priori* sop, a mere declaration of official objectives in the guise of a statement of their attainment. I have questioned the framework of these objectives, but it is even doubtful that the legal system does all that much to protect life and property. The deterrence value of legal terrosism, for example, is deeply questioned in a quaker monograph on the prison system: *Struggle for Justice*, (Hill and Wang, New York, 1971), which concludes its sceptical chapter on deterrence with the remark that:

> At the beginning of this study we emphasised that criminal justice is inextricably interwoven with social justice. To this tangled skein we must now add a new complication: a fair, equal and rational system of criminal justice can only be achieved by a society of such maturity and self-confidence that it no longer needs to use criminals as scapegoats on which to load its angers and frustrations. (p. 60-1)

Here the authors are drawing attention to the interconnections between the 'protective' role of criminal punishment and the vicious form that it takes. For even if Hart and Morris and the others were justified in depicting our society's

laws as just and in depicting our society as one in which
'mutual benefit' were the everyday reality, so that crime
would indeed be a violation of something basically good, it
would still be a gross distortion to depict the 'price' and
'penalty' system by which criminals 'pay their debt to society', namely the prisons, in the whitewashing and legitimating terms in which they do depict them. For if our society
were a humane one, it would not deal in a brutal way with
those who violate its values. So, having questioned the
background behind the standard rationalisations of 'punishment', I want to draw attention to some features of this
practice not often attend to: those features namely, which
exist.

Every sentence is in order as it is. Prisons and Punishment.
Like Hart, Morris and Edgar Lustgarden of the B.B.C.'s
crime-and-punishment stories, many conceive of punishment
in the terms of a 'payment', and it may be that years and
months constitute a kind of measure of negative currency, a
quantity of payment. But if you push Morris's 'exacting the
debt' locution, it is evident that, unknown to him, it must be a
metaphor, since, whereas the payment of a literal debt does
actually accrue to the creditor, no such paying back, retribution, occurs when someone does time in prison. On the
contrary, despite slave labour, the prisons are a massive
financial and manpower burden to 'the taxpaying public'. In
societies where, by contrast, the 'paying back' is a more
literal phenomenon, namely in many tribal societies, the
methods of dealing with wrong-doing are vastly different
from imprisonment, the first experience of which is to native
peoples an experience of incredible barbarity, (See Malinowski: *Crime and Custom in Savage Society*, 1962 and
Gluckman: *Politics, Law and Ritual in Tribal Society,* 1965.)
Commonly, within such cultures, the doing of a wrong is
something that, by disturbing the networks of reciprocity,
necessitates material and symbolic restoration (necessarily
involving suffering and thus 'punishment') of harmony, a
restoration in which all are involved and in which the climax
is the reconciliation of wrongdoer and wronged. 'Punishment' in our culture, annihilates relationships; in some

cultures what we call by the same name has the opposite tendency.

Now it may be that 'retribution' in its western sense can only be understood in the theocentric terms of the Judaic and Christian tradition, in terms of a payment to God, the Great Debt-Collector in The Sky. Certainly we ought to find the practices that go under the heading 'punishment' deeply puzzling (at least) and not to be passed off in a pseudo-self-explanatory officialese. Prisons, for example, only emerged to dominate the punitive landscape in the modern era; and, especially in Bentham's writings and in the rather different writings and practices of the penitentiary-builders of early nineteenth-century New York and Pennsylvania, specific 'philosophies of imprisonment' were propounded and acted on, philosophies which drew on the judao-christian tradition but adapted it specifically to 'modern needs'. Bentham's 'panopticon' was originally designed as a factory, and Bentham indeed advocated that the prisons, functioning as hell below the purgatory of the work-houses, would be factories, not only in producing goods at a profit (to the overseers) but in publicly embodying the compulsion to labour. Thus, through the provision of places for people, unseen by the inmates, to witness the spectacular sufferings and arduous fate of those who had shirked honest labour, the prisons were spectacularly to reinforce, in an instructive entertainment for all the family, the virtues essential to a developing capitalist society (see *Works*, Vol. I, p. 498). We shall see in later chapters how all this fits into Bentham's overall philosophy. The panopticon was not built, but philosophy had more success in America where, according to de Tocqueville, 'they have caught the monomania of the penitentiary system which seems to them the remedy for all evils of society'. In his book *The Discovery of the Asylum* (Boston, 1972), David Rothman writes:

> Proponents described the penitentiary as 'a grand theatre, for the trial of all new plans in hygiene and education, in physical and moral reform'. The convict 'surrendered body and soul to be experimented on' and the results, as the Boston Prison Discipline Society insisted... 'would greatly promote order, seriousness and purity in large families, male and female,

boarding schools and colleges'... the Reverend James B.
Finley, chaplain at the Ohio penitentiary... declared 'Could we
all be put on prison fare, for the space of two or three
generations, the world would ultimately be the better for it.
Indeed, should society change places with the prisoners, so far
as habits are concerned, taking to itself the regularity and
temperance and sobriety of a good prison', then the grand
goals of peace, production, right and Christianity would be
furthered. 'As it is', concluded Finley, 'taking this world and
the next together... the prisoner has the advantage'. (pp. 84-5)

With great perspicacity, and thinking almost wholly in a
deterministic frame of reference, the penitentiary builders
saw their task as providing the 'moral architecture' of a society
which as it industrialised, had an unprecedented need for a
sober temperate, and regular workforce, and, at the same
time, through the growth of factories and urban concentr-
ations, was losing precisely the traditional 'mechanisms' for
producing that discipline: the close patriarchial family and
the disciplining bonds of the small community. In this light,
they saw the criminal essentially as someone who had not
undergone moralisation but had, by a natural process, fallen
into the easy, vicious ways of urban life. State supervision,
and especially imprisonment, therefore, were the means
whereby this influence could be undone and the moral
training missed in childhood and youth provided by a kind of
second upbringing. Rothman describes the Pennsylvania
system:

The arrangements at the Philadelphia prison, as partisans
described them, guaranteed that convicts would avoid all
contamination and follow a path to reform. Inmates remained
in solitary cells for eating, sleeping and working, and entered
private yards for exercise; they saw and spoke with only
carefully selected visitors, and read only morally uplifting
literature - the Bible. Officials placed hoods over the head of a
new prisoner when marching him to his cell so he could not see
or be seen by other inmates... Left in total solitude, separated
from 'evil society... the progress of corruption is arrested; no
additional contamination can be received or communicated'...
the convict 'will be compelled to reflect on the error of his
ways, to listen to the reproaches of his conscience... Then,
after a period of total isolation, without companions, books,

tools, officials would allow the inmate to work in the cell. Introduced at this moment, labour would become not an oppressive task for punishment, but a welcome diversion... regularity and discipline would become habitual. He would return to the community cured of vice and idleness, to take his place as a responsible citizen'. (*Discovery*, pp. 85-6)

Jessica Mitford, acknowledging *Struggle for Justice*, incisively traces this fantasy-mongering down to the Skinnerian present in her *The American Prison Business* (Pelican, 1977). Comparisons and contrasts are suggested by Mihajlo Mihajlov's 'Dostoevsky's and Solzhenitsyn's *House of the Dead*' in *Russian Themes* (London, 1968) and by Bao-Ruo-wang (Jean Pasqualini) and Rudolph Chelminski in *Prisoner of Mao* (Pelican, 1974). On British prisons I have found valuable Mike Fitzgerald's *Prisoners in Revolt* (Pelican, 1977), and U.R.Q. Henriques' 'The Rise and Decline of the Separate System of Prison Discipline', in *Past and Present* No. 54, 1976).

No more than crime, then, can punishment be treated in the abstract; rather do we have to look at specific practices with specific histories, ideologies and effects. If we don't look at that, if we concentrate only on the official and rhetorical 'language of punishment', we will be drawn on the one hand into false antitheses, as for example between 'punishment', which, according to Hart, Morris and others 'respects' the responsibility of the criminal, and 'treatment', which deals with people as though they were 'sick animals' to be manipulated. Now, while not denying that real and important problems are being raised here, what I would want to stress is that these philosophers, aloof from the experience either of guarding or being guarded, fail to concern themselves with the 'rationalising' character of so much of this debate; for the overwhelming reality brought out in detail in the books I have cited is that 'punishment' is brutally manipulative and 'treatment' viciously punitive. A kick in the head takes its toll whether given by a guard's boot or by a doctor's electrodes:

> Although punishment is no longer a fashionable rationale for criminal justice, the punitive spirit has survived unscathed behind the mask of treatment. (*Struggle for Justice*, p. 26)

The authors go on to argue that the basic function of the 'treatment philosophy', with its notion of crime as a 'sympton of inadequacy in the total personality', is to legitimate, in the context of a mounting crisis of authority, the escalation of surveillance, authority, coercion and conrol, and to remove the justification of prison practices to the unchallengeable authority of certified experts. It is, I think, possible and important to develop a concept of 'therapy' which does not violate agency or autonomy, but which precisely seeks to enhance these. Similarly it is possible to show that determinism does not necessarily consign human beings to the status of passive victims of their situation but can embrace an understanding of them responding actively to their situation in terms of their perceptions and reasonings. It is not 'determinism' or 'the therapeutic model' (as against 'free will' and 'desert') that are the key to the problem, however, for what is overwhelming is the euphemistic and rationalising motivation of the rhetoric. Hence it is only in terms of an attempt to understand the practices rationalised that the rhetoric can be properly evaluated. Here is *Struggle for Justice's* summary of those realities, a summary that echoes a hundred prison memoirs:

> Where 'progressive penology' rules, the changes are trivial when measured against penal coercion's human cost. We submit that the basic evils of imprisonment are that it denies autonomy, degrades dignity, impairs or destroys self-reliance, inculcates authoritarian values, minimises the likelihood of beneficial interaction with one's peers, fractures family ties, destroys the family's economic stability, and prejudices the prisoner's future prospects for any improvement in his economic and social status. It does all these things whether or not the buildings are antiseptic or dirty, the aroma that of fresh bread or stale urine, the sleeping accommodation a plank or an inner-spring matress, or the interaction of inmates takes place in cells and corridors ('idleness') or in the structural setting of a particular time and place ('group therapy'). (p. 33)

Kropotkin had written in a similar vein:

> No matter what changes are introduced in the prison regime, the problem of second offenders does not decrease. That is inevitable;—it must be so;—the prison kills all the qualities in a

man which make him best adapted to community life. It makes
him the kind of person who will return to prison to end his days
in one of those stone tombs over which is engraved—'House of
Correction and Detention'. There is only one answer to the
question: 'What can be done to better this penal system?'
Nothing. A prison cannot be improved. With the exception of a
few unimportant little improvements, there is absolutely
nothing to do but demolish it. (*Pamplets*, 'Prisons and their
Moral Influence on Prisoners' p. 33): (Kropotkin does not seem
to have envisaged the impact of prisoners' rights movements
reforming from below.)

If people want to defend the *status quo*, let them defend it
and not some 'position' merely assumed to correspond to the
status quo. It is doubtful to what extent prisons have a serious
deterrent effect. It is certain that they are, as Kropotkin says,
'schools of crime'. Since the bulk of even officially designated
criminals are at large, prisons can have but a marginal
protective role in society, even ignoring the fact that they
make more dangerous those they process. Since, despite this,
it is doubtful that more than a small percentage of prisoners
are so dangerously disposed in the first place to constitute a
social menace, it is certain that, in 'the economics of violence', prisons do more violence than they prevent. If there
are people who constitute a standing menace to their fellows,
it may be that in the event of the impossibility of coping with
them at large, they can justifiably be sequestrated in places,
'prisons', if you like, whose sole function would be to
'contain' them; that is, 'punishment' would not be the aim
and they would have adequate comforts and company consistent with security. But, commenting on such a proposal,
Jessica Mitford warns against not going the whole abolition-
ist hog and presents the problem thus:

> somebody has to decide who is dangerous... and there is no
> consensus among judges as to who is 'dangerous'... For the
> same offence, one judge would have given probation; another
> twenty years in the penitentiary. (*Prison Business*, p. 313)

A penal philosophy, implicitly or explicitly, embodies a
total social philosophy; and similarly penal practices can only
be understood in the context of social practices in which they

have their meaning and role. Our prison system, for all its genuine terroristic effect, is in large measure a fetish, a token, a ritual, which lulls 'respectable' people with incantations of 'maintaining law and order' at the expense of victimising a tiny minority of wrongdoers and deviants unlucky enough to be trapped into a hell on earth—a festival of the repressed at the expense of the oppressed. If you oppose it, it is necessary to see this in the context of a revolutionary opposition to the crime and chaos that passes for law-and-order in capitalist society. That means working for a society where people will not be structurally propelled towards doing each other in and where people will not be driven to rob, rape, or kill to attain comfort, status, or power.

CHAPTER 4

MORALISM AND MORALITY

Moral Philosophy in the Academy

As taught and practised in our universities, 'Moral Philosophy' ('Ethics') is an arid affair, earnest without being serious,
individualistic without being personal, conventional without
being social, and formal without being structural. The courses are usually compulsory for philosophy students, and it is in
the spirit of compulsive duty that they are typically taught
and taken. After a long period when, in accordance with the
doctrine of emotivism and subjectivism, substantial moral
argument was banned as intrinsically sub-rational, there are
signs in the journals that philosophers are timidly emerging
to air their thoughts on some of life's questions. But this is
less the case in Britain, where topics like 'Weakness of Will'
remain as close to the bone as most like to come, than in the
more disturbed culture of the United States. Whether or not
British philosophers might be prepared at a price to discuss
such things as violence or abortion with their colleagues, or in
an occasional talk to a society, they are very reluctant to
bring such difficult and controversial matters up in front of
the children - 'that would only confuse them'. Great Books,
from Plato to Mill, provide the backbone of the syllabus. But,
under a pervasively formalistic definition of philosophy,
which abstracts 'analysis' from its traditional place in philosophers' struggles to develop a coherent vision of the world
they live in, the books are first snatched from their context
and then plucked, gutted, boned and canned to suit the
parochial culinary capacities of the domestic academic chefs.
Little wonder perhaps, that philosophers professionally committed to ignoring the substantial backgrounds, 'philosophies
of life', behind different moral theories and views, are prone
to espouse formalistic views as to the nature of morality.

Facts and Values
Some orthodox academics are aware that all is not well. In
Contemporary Moral Philosophy (Macmillan, 1967), G.J.
Warnock remarks on the 'remarkably barren' character of
twentieth-century, Anglo-American moral philosophy (p.
1). Writing within the analytical school of his targets (Moore,
Ayer, Stevenson and Hare), Warnock succeeds in exposing
their shortcomings. In particular he shows the failure of these
people in their aim to give an account of moral language in
terms of its functional and formal features: expressing or
inducing feelings, expressing or enjoining universal practical
commitments. What Warnock argues, and his later book *The
Object of Morality* (Methuen, 1971) attempts to develop the
idea, is that moral language can only be understood in terms
not just of feelings or volitions but of beliefs, purporting to
be true, about human life and human activity. Thus he
argues, broadly reasserting the empiricist utilitarianism of
the traditional British Moralists, that morality has to be
understood in terms of a more or less determinate content: in
terms of human welfare and harm. Like Philippa Foot (see
her article in *Theories of Ethics*, O.U.P., 1967), then,
Warnock, with all sorts of disclaimers reestablishes 'naturalism', so superficially scorned by the mainstream of recent
academic ethics. Perhaps now it will be less common for
Moral Philosophy lecture courses to open with a warning to
students not to think of moral philosophy as having any
'business' advocating moral views or inculcating moral
wisdom ('whatever that expression might turn out to mean'),
as if arguing for a moral view were inherently indoctrinating.
The anti-naturalists had set out to mark off moral 'talk' from
the more intellectually respectable language of empirical fact
accessible to proper scientific investigation. Rejecting, moreover, Moore's 'institutionism', which placed moral truths on a
pedestal *above* ordinary facts, they demoted morality to the
level of more or less blind (albeit deeply held) feelings and
choices. Thus the scope for evidence and reasoning in
morality is by these writers logically circumscribed, no
substantial consideration about the nature of things being
essentially relevant to the case. We should note the *a priori*
casualness with which the doctrine was supported, for it tells

us a lot about the contempt for experience and thought that is none too rare among the cloistered empiricists and unthinking rationalists of Academe.

A.J. Ayer in *Language, Truth and Logic* (Gollancz, 1935) presents as a 'typical example' of moral argument: 'a man said that thrift was a virtue and another replied that it was a vice' (p. 110). He goes on that, in so far as this is a conflict over 'question of value' it is no factual disagreement. We are, then, supposed to imagine this 'typical' situation, a situation in which, if he is denying that at least some thrift is necessary in this world, someone seems to be saying something quite insane. Perhaps the disputants are not operating with the same idea of what thrift is, perhaps they have different views as to the role of saving in life, perhaps one is a peasant, the other a playboy; we, Ayer's readers, do not know, and hence the possibility of understanding what might be at issue is foreclosed. But, since Ayer uses this example to justify his emotive subjectivism, he would need to establish his claim that the question of thrift's value cannot be answered by an understanding of concrete human conditions and dispositions. The naturalist is not committed to the idea that the truth or falsity of moral propositions can be decided on immediate inspection. Nor need he think that all moral questions, any more than all questions of physics or psychology, are within our capacity to answer definitively at all.

Charles Stevenson, claiming in *Ethics and Language* (Yale 1944) to base on 'observation' his 'emotive' theory (that moral words like 'good' have meaning only in so far as they function to elicit feelings - so that they are pious sisters of pornography), makes similar use of one of the few 'examples' to be found in his book. He presents the following:

> The trustees for the estate of a philanthropist have been instructed to forward any charitable cause that seems to them worthy. One suggests that they provide hospital facilities for the poor, the other that they endow universities. (p. 13)

Insofar as the case is clear, many might feel the answer obvious; but like most philosophers 'examples', Stevenson's is hopelessly indeterminate, and its indeterminacy, precisely by precluding any possibility of a sound judgement (suppose university research, unusually enough, was making important contributions to the health of 'the poor'), lends a spurious credibility to Stevenson's line. But it is worse than that: for Stevenson, thinking of his academic and well-meaning audience, deliberately presents it with a dilemma - a choice between two wonderful things - and it is obvious that to a true dilemma there is no 'right' answer. But the dilemma presupposes for its polemical force the very thing that Stevenson uses the example to deny. For it is only because the case is accepted as one of competing but really good options that readers feel the lack of a correct solution. Such dilemmas can arise in any field: in the development of scientific hypotheses and in the selection of football teams. They show that not all questions have a simple answer, not that they are pseudo-questions. And the same point applies to Hare's introductory example in *Freedom and Reason* (Oxford, 1963) where, following Sartre, he poses for us the vicarious choice between caring for one's mother or joining a guerilla struggle against the Nazis. The example is used to show that moral principles are essentially a matter of (solemn) choice. But they no more establish that than would an intractable problem of psychological interpretation show that understanding people is essentially a matter of choice. Again, a lazy subjectivism is encouraged - and of course, it is very useful to those whose laziness extends to practical matters to be able to turn every moral issue into a nice dilemma!

These points merely reinforce Warnock's criticisms. But what is interesting about his books (as well as what is boring about them!) is that over-conscious, perhaps of the weight of orthodoxy, Warnock does not seek to explore the 'content' of morality, the nature of human 'welfare', much beyond noting, truly enough, that to addict children to heroin would be a bad thing (*Contemporary Moral Philosophy*, p. 70) and that 'non-maleficence, fairness, beneficence and non-deception' are, in the general run of life's circumstances, good dispositions (*Object of Morality*, p. 86). Nor does he explore the idea, so grotesquely caricatured in the 'anti-naturalist' writers' view of moral statements as 'imperatives', that morality needs to be understood, partly at least, in terms of 'form', of social and psychological 'structures'. Warnock gives us a functional account of morality in terms of its role in making the 'human predicament' less grim than, in a quasi-Hobbesian state of nature, it seems inherently liable to be and to do so specifically by seeking to countervail the deleterious liabilities inherent in 'limited sympathies' (*Object*, p. 86), so that it disposes people to act 'otherwise than people are just naturally disposed to do' (*Object*, p. 76). But Warnock leaves mysterious the source of this convenient 'desideratum' and of its power and energy to perform what *ex hypothesi* appears as a miracle, since the very things (human viciousness) that create the need for morality seem to preclude it. No wonder the moralists of old dragged God and the afterlife in at about this point! We can begin to see perhaps that the 'imperativist' theory of Professor Hare, however mistaken as an analysis of the meaning of moral 'utterances', does reflect the way in which 'morality' is typically experienced, namely as a quasi-external command and as a prohibition against natural impulse (see R. Norman: 'Moral Philosophy without Moraity?' *Radical Philosophy 6*, 1973). Statism psychologised!

Liberal authoritarianism

Now, what goes on in philosophy departments, though it might earn knighthoods, does not earn headlines in the national media. Nonetheless, it would be foolish to deny that academic philosophers' doctrines do play a role in national culture and politics, reinforcing as well as reflecting the currents they articulate. A vast number of politicians and bureaucrats go through philosophy courses, especially at Oxford. Social scientists meekly quake lest a philosopher catch them leaping across the fact/value fence; and of course schoolteachers absorb the received philosophical wisdom in a hand-me-down form at their training colleges. Whatever the causal connection here, it is certainly the case in my experience, as a teacher in the spiritual sanctuaries that are our universities, that many students arrive disposed, as I was, to propound and accept the philosophy that Warnock and Philippa Foot tried to undermine. They are often confirmed subjectivists, to whom the idea of a *true* moral belief is as absurd as the idea of a square circle. Yet they appear 'well brought up', well 'morally trained' by their family and school backgrounds, despite disavowing the full-blown version of the sunday-school pieties in terms of which this training was received. On the face of it at least, their subjectivism tends to have little iconoclastic or rebellious about it: they voice, for example, little resentment at the daily dose of authoritarian religiosity in whose name they have been domesticated—that would be 'fanatical'. So 'liberal' are many of my students indeed, that they hold that it is immoral to 'pass moral judgement on people'—as this would involve the 'judge' in 'setting himself up as a moral authority'. But it is the specific 'form' of the moral judgement that seems central. My students agree without exception that it would, in fact, be a very bad thing for one of them to be injured in a landslide. So I ask them whether it would not, by the same token, be a very bad thing (in fact) for someone to bring such an injury about, deliberately or through negligence. If it is a bad thing to happen, surely it must be a bad thing to bring about... They reply: 'One is a medical fact, the other a moral assumption'. So, and overwhelmingly, whereas injuries are seen as quite unmysterious empirical and 'natural' evils, criticising the effecting human agency as evil is seen as indulging personal, or religious, or conventional 'attitudes'. Such are the effects it seems to me of an authoritarian education and the authoritarian conception of morality that it communicates. Morality is identified with the unquestioning acceptance of some internal or external authority, and emancipation and the adoption of a 'liberal' posture is felt to entail the unquestioning avoidance of 'moral judgements' and the adoption, therefore, of an uncritical and indifferent outlook. This subjectivism bifurcates even within an individual's mind, in ways that are reflected by the difference in moral psychology implicit in the difference between the Ayer-Stevenson 'emotive' theory on one hand, and the Hare 'imperative' theory on the other. On one hand 'the moral' is seen to reside in the private breasts of individuals, at the level of their 'personal feelings' about things: to endeavour to persuade another, let alone to coerce him or her, is 'just to impose your values on them'. On the other hand 'morality' is seen to reside at the level of 'norms' by which 'society' induces conformity in individuals — imposition, then, far from violating morality, is seen as of its very essence. In either case, whether seen as a private conviction or as public institution, whether as a matter of sentiment or as a matter of convention and conditioning, morality is 'relative'. Thus, in my experience, students tend to hover between a merely formal libertarianism ('Live by your own values') and a purely formal collectivism ('It depends what is right in your own particular society'). This dichotomy of individual freedom and social constraint is of course as old as the sophists Plato argued with and as deeply entrenched as the bourgeois social order - the apostles of free enterprise are one and the same as the spokesmen of 'law and order'! And you have only to read the recent moral tracts of Oxford philosophers, P.F. Strawson's 'Social Morality and Individual Ideals' (*Philosophy*, 1961), and Stuart Hampshire's '*Morality and Pessimism*' (Cambridge, 1972) - see my 'Wadham Warden Warns World' in *Radical Philosophy* 5 - to find this dichotomy, this bourgeois idea of society as a set of cages within which we can do our own thing without tearing each other apart: this idea of society as a well-policed market.

Morality, then, has the same social function as the law in Hart's scheme of things, and its means, the 'internal barriers' which prevent 'impermissible conduct' (Hampshire), appear none too different from the more 'physical' methods of the law. Yet Hart himself, in *Law, Liberty and Moraity* (Oxford, 1962) embraces the private sentimental pole on which to hang 'morality', so that he can defend 'purely private' conduct to which there are 'merey moral' objections, such as homosexual relations, from the law. Thus Hart's case against the authoritarian Lord Devlin (*The Enforcement of Morals*, Oxford, 1965), does not transcend J.S. Mill's dichotomy of individual freedom and social constraint because Hart is unable to mount a defence of homosexual rights in terms which grant the sexual freedom has to be defended as a social freedom with social repurcussions: for the family, for example, as Devlin clearly sees. Instead Hart is confined to talking of moral questions as 'no business of society' and hence by the same argument to concede that anything which can be seen as society's business, is fair game for legal prohibition (... but as long as homosexuals don't make public exhibitions of themselves and a long as prostitutes stay off the streets...). My students are in good company: their liberal dualisms can be found articulated by the finest minds in the academy.

So the student is likely to emerge from his Moral Philosophy cocoon not transformed, but merely decorated. Her assumptions about 'facts and values' and about 'the individual and society' are unlikely to have been challenged, while the chances of his having there examined any real-life moral question are remote. Well has it been said, therefore, that the serious student with philosophic bent might be better occupied studying literature or sociology than undergoing the conventional 'Ethics' course. Moral thought involves reflection on human social experience, and moral philosophy may be characterised as an attempt to understand critically the most general categories of that experience. But, as social experience is not monolithic, as it involves disparities and especially tensions and conflicts, as social experience is 'political', it is misleading to think of moral philosophy as setting out to clarify 'the' or 'our' concept of morality. I have already indicated the instability in my students' ground-floor sense of the 'seat' of morality - in the individual's heart or in the society's rules? — and it seems to me that such instabilities embody unstable visions of human social life. What needs to be done, then, is to examine and criticise inadequate conceptions of morality in terms of an examination and criticism of the human social vision they embody and the human and social reality they articulate, reflect, and reinforce. This means that, before coming back to examine and perhaps replace the framework of our moral philosophers, we have to stray beyond the groves of academe into the jungles of social reality. Let us begin with Marx.

The Bureaucrat and the Beast: The Dualities of Moralism

Marx and Morality

Marx spoke with contempt of morality, is said to have burst out laughing at the mention of the word, and claimed (in *The*

German Ideology) 'the Communists preach no morality at all'. Yet it is obvious that Marx knew capitalism to be a vicious social order, at best transitionally necessary, in favourable conditions to be overthrown and replaced by a better one, socialism, which would in turn evolve into communist society. Most commentators have seen inconsistency here; even the orthodox have offered psychological explanations. Some say: 'Of course ethics is at the root of Marxism, but Marx's own bewitchment by the prevailing positivist ideology of 'science' led him to conceal it'. Others say: 'Of course moral principles have nothing in common with Marxist science and Marxist politics, whose task is simply to advance the objective interests of the working class'. Still others say: 'Of course, *as a science* Marxism is value-free; but Marxist *praxis* presupposes extra-empirical commitment to socialist ideals'. And so, scholastic refinements daily emerging, the debate among professional Marxists goes on (see Lucien Goldmann's 'Is there a Marxist Sociology?' reprinted in *Radical Philosophy* 1). There are textual sources for all of these interpretations (thus the irony of the sectarian 'of courses'), but it is possible to see that Marx's condemnation of capitalism is quite consistent with his contempt for morality.

Unlike Kautsky (*Ethics and the Materialist Interpretation of History*) and Engels (*Anti-Dühring*) Marx appears to have had a quite specific conception of morality; he did not see the term generically as embracing the 'norms and values' of any historical society. For him, morality was an historically fairly specific ideological institution, functioning to mystify and discipline people in accordance with the oppressive needs of class society. He did not argue for a 'socialist morality'; rather he claimed that the communist movement 'shatters the basis of all morality' (*German Ideology*). To the class-conscious proletarian 'law, morality and religion are... so many bourgeois prejudices behind which there lurk in ambush just as many bourgeois interests' (*Communist Manifesto*).

But clearly, whether 'young' or 'mature', Marx wrote of capitalism as an evil social order whatever its 'progressive' aspects. In *Capital,* Volume 1, for example, he says:

Within the capitalist system all methods for raising the social productiveness of labour are brought about at the cost of the individual labourer; all means for the development of production transform themselves into means of domination over and exploitation of the producers; they mutilate the labourer into a fragment of a man, degrade him to the level of an appendage to a machine, destroy every remnant of charm in his work and turn it into hated toil; they estrange from him the intellectual potentialities of the labour process in the same proportion as science is incorporated in it as an independent power; they distort the conditions under which he works, subject him during the labour process to a despotism the more hateful for its meanness; they transform his life-time into working-time, and drag his wife and child beneath the wheels of the juggernaut of capital. But all methods for the production of surplus-value are at the same time methods of accumulation; and every extension of accumulation becomes again a means for the development of those methods. It follows, therefore, that in proportion as capital accumulates, the lot of the labourer, be his payment high or low, must grow worse. (Moscow Edition, p. 645)

Why is this attack on capitalism consistent with the rejection of 'the moral point of view'? Because 'morality' is in his view, one of the real evils of capitalist society. What is the nature of this evil?

The first point I would make is that it is not the specific content of specifically bourgeois moral ideas that is centrally at issue here; I mean: ideas about the sanctity of private property, the family, and the state. Obviously Marxists are going to debunk such ideas as masks over capitalism's inhuman face. But Marx is not advocating that socialists work out a system of moral principles which do not consecrate bourgeois social relations. He is not concerned, then, to promulgate non-invidious moral commandments such as 'treat no one as a means', or 'tell the truth', in the manner of a radical follower of Kant. For such left-philanthropists assume that, perhaps with divine help, obedience to such imperatives would in fact serve the common good, serve mankind. But whereas, unlike 'respect your boss's property', the Kantian imperatives do not have an invidious content, and may even provide the terms of social criticism and in the

name of the higher authority of conscience command rebellion, blanket obedience to them, here and now, supports
exploitation and deception. For to refrain on principle from
harming, or lying to, the bosses or the officers of the state is
to consent to exploitation by those whose good is typically the
harm of the exploited. To fall for the cry of 'let us all make
sacrifices for the good of all' , is to be played for a fool; there
is scant common good.

But I do not think it is a question for Marx of rejecting or
replacing such norms with revolutionary socialist norms.
(Compare E. Kamenka, *The Ethical Foundations of Marxism*, London, 1962.) Trotsky proposes such a replacement in
his debate with Dewey (see *Their Morals and Ours*, Merit,
N.Y., 1966). Having attacked the hypocrisy of bourgeois
morality and the futility of Kantian philanthropism, Trotsky
puts forward a set of moral imperatives geared to revolutionary politics as understood within the Leninist framework.
He advocates, in fact, a socialist utilitarianism, advocating
duties and sacrifices subservient to the end of 'increasing the
power of man over nature and abolishing the power of man
over man'. What he does then, is alter the content of moral
ideas, setting out socialist principles instead of bourgeois
ones (see also Lenin's *Address to the Third All-Russian
Congress of Communist Youth*, 1920, an important and
oft-reprinted bible of Soviet Moralistianity). But whether such
codes are called 'socialist morality' or 'truly human morality',
they ignore, or even suppress, questions of the 'structure' or
'form' of morality, questions of whether the 'content' of
socialist ideals admits of realisation through a practice of
submission to duty, however much such practices may sometimes confront the *status quo*. Such thinking remains within
the conceptual framework of bourgeois moralism. The best
explicit statement of such an incomplete break that I know is
Bertrand Russell's in his *Marriage and Morals* (Unwin, 1929,
1972 impression):

> Conventional morality has erred, not in demanding self-
> control, but in demanding it in the wrong place. (p. 120)

Despite much of Russell's drift, then, he here affirms that
his concern is simply with content; he does not question the

different forms of 'self-control' (taboo, inhibition). It was not this sort of road, I think, that Marx was concerned to point. He called the whole established notion and practice of 'morality' into question. Not concerning himself with the positive task of outlining a socialist 'structure' appropriate to a socialist 'content', of developing a more adequate *concept* of morality, Marx regarded morality as he regarded religion, as inherently ideological, mystifying and repressive. We have seen how radicals might think it adequate to put forward new moral principles for old, and we need to explore the common structural core and the common 'psychological politics' that these different systems share with established bourgeois moral thought and practice.

I begin with an account of what I see as fundamentally dualistic categories of moralism as articulated and as criticised in philosophy books, sermons, tracts and popular media. I shall then attempt to locate this discourse as reflecting, characterising and reinforcing class and specifically capitalist social relations. Then I shall try to portray the institutional transmission and embodiment of 'morality', thus understood, within our society - 'moral education'. From that point I propose to outline an alternative categorial scheme, social form, and mode of education in such a way as to bring out the connection between an adequate notion of morality and a radical social vision. In short, I shall try to help rescue the concept of morality from the jaws of moralism.

Durkheim: socialisation, coercion and morality

In *Moral Education* (Free Press, N.Y., 1973), Emile Durkheim, the father of modern sociology wrote:

> Morality is the totality of definite rules; it is like so many moulds with limiting boundaries into which we must pour our behaviour... the function of morality is, in the first place, to determine conduct, to fix it, to eliminate the element of individual arbitrariness. Doubtless the content of moral precepts, that is to say the nature of the prescribed behaviour also has moral value and we shall discuss this. However, since all such precepts promote regularity of conduct among men, there is a moral aspect in that these actions - not only in their specific content but in a general way - are held to contain regularity. That is why transients and people who cannot hold themselves

to specific jobs are always suspect. It is because their moral
temperament is fundamentally defective—because it is most
uncertain and undependable. (pp. 26-7)

Durkheim goes on to depict the means whereby these
disciplining boundaries can most effectively be established
within the soul, so that, even when the backs of authorities,
uniformed or otherwise, are turned, the individual, 'moralised', 'socialised', will police himself.

Morality, then, according to this bourgeois picture, is
'self-control'; but between the self who controls and the self
who is controlled there is a gulf, a gulf as wide as that between
a bestial state-of-nature and an ordered society, and a gulf as
narrow, since the forces of anarchy ever threaten to over-
whelm their internal ruler. Morality is the political 'problem
of order' as it is solved in the head, and the long process of
moral education is the authoritarian struggle to achieve that
solution. Morality's target, then, is the baseness that is at the
core of man's natural, unimproved, state; a baseness which
consists, if not necessarily in the outright wickedness that
John Wesley attributed even to young children, in blind
wilfulness, savage wildness, thoughtless destructiveness, and
indulgent selfishness. Morality's function, then, is precisely
to inhibit, discipline, control, suppress, these impulses,
inclinations, passions, instincts, and thus to guide us in the
paths, if not of outright righteousness, at least of common
decency. The moral man, the man of character, through the
prodding of prickling power of his conscience, is able thus to
regulate his conduct. As Professor Richard Peters puts it:

> Character-traits are internalised social rules such as honesty,
> punctuality, truthfulness and unselfishness. A person's char-
> acter represents his own achievement, his own manner of
> imposing regulation upon his inclinations. (*Ethics and Educ-
> ation*, Allen and Unwin, 1966, p. 57)

If moral action occurs in the outer social world, it is the
inner private world that is the locus of the moral drama. For it
is within the individual breast that the moralist locates the
forces of good and evil. Thus it is individuals' success or
failure in self-control that is the key to social well-being or
discord. There is evil in the world, we are to believe, because

there are unmoralised individuals in the world: inside agitators; and evil will be kept down to the extent that such bad
agents are suppressed or caused to repent and to suppress
themselves. Thus, according to our moral judges, it is 'up to
the individual' to discipline himself, to measure up to 'what is
required'. If he fails to do this, it is his fault and he is to
blame. As the cause of his own shortcoming he must, 'if he
has any conscience at all', change himself. This whole
voluntaristic claptrap amounts to the demand that individuals lift themselves up by their own spiritual bootlaces. The
high moral tone of this individualistic voluntarianism masks
its function as the social mobilisation of fear; but this
mobilisation becomes quite explicit when judges, while
abusing the transgressor for his culpably vicious mind, attributes blame, out of the side of their mouth (addressing 'the
authorities'), to the 'permissive climate of our times'. The
moralist puns on 'responsibility'. He says: 'the child must be
held responsible before he *is* responsible, so that he may
become responsible'. Removing the play on words we might
say that the child is to be punished before he knows what he is
doing so that he will come to obey voluntarily, to be moral.
As Nietzsche said:

> Men were treated as free so that they might be judged and
> punished, so that they might become guilty. (*Twilight of the
> Idols'*, *The Portable Nietzsche*; ed. Kauffman, Viking, 1964, p.
> 499)

Moralists thus try to get us to see the source both of our
ruin and of our salvation as within our own selves. They are
concerned to present us to ourselves as cut off, not only from
direct social communication, but from direct social determination. Basic to this thought is the split between people, so
that it is only through moral compulsion or other external
forces that we will be sociable. Durkheim's very definition of
society is in terms of its 'externality' and 'coerciveness' with
respect to society's individual members (*Rules of Sociological
Method*, Macmillan, 1964, p. 2). And equally basic, since
implanted compelling conscience is at war with innate,
rebellious impulse, is the split within the individual.

Morality, then, has the mystical function of joining together what natural inclination would burst apart. Morality, rational, disinterested, universal, enters as a *deus ex machina* as *that-which-overcometh* our capricious, selfish, particularistic defects, as the mysterious, self-composed, internal cement which holds all together by holding each down. It is the internal referee that ensures that the social contest is fairly fought. The conscience is the statesman of the soul.

Kant and moral jewellery

It is the writings of Kant that express most clearly this wholesale dualism. He held human beings capable only of capricious and sporadic direct inclinations towards each other; he harped on the 'slavish', 'blind', 'animal' nature of all inclinations, whether sociable or not, and was prone to depict 'giving in' to impulses such as sympathy or liking as just as self-indulgent as giving in to any other inclination:

> delight in the satisfaction of others... however amiable... is on a level with other inclinations, e.g. the inclination to honour... (*Fundamental Principles of the Metaphysics of Ethics*, transl. Abbott, Longmans, 1955, p. 16).

Though occasionally, and through 'accident' or 'coincidence', such inclinations might issue in actions 'in accordance with duty', their general tendency is to lead us away from duty's strict path:

> since man is acted upon by so many inclinations that, though capable of the idea of pure practical reason, he is not so easily able to make it effective *in concreto* in his life. (*Fundamental Principles*, p. 5)

Thus, duty, the commandment of pure practical reason, dictates the control of inclination and the pursuit of virtue quite independent of inclination:

> Thus, e.g., I ought to endeavour to promote the happiness of others, not as if its realization involved any concern of mine (whether by immediate inclination or by any satisfaction gained indirectly through reason), but simply because a maxim which excludes it cannot be comprehended as a natural law in one and the same volition. (*Fundamental Principles,* p. 72)

The moral man, then acts under constraints; yet since it is a constraint imposed on him (his inclinations) by Himself (his

Reason), the moral act is, *par excellence,* a 'free' act.

> A free will and a will subject to moral laws are one and the same. (Fundamental Principles, p. 79 (Abbott).)

> Yet this freedom is opposed to vulgar spontaneity or common humanity:

> For men and all rational creatures, the moral necessity is a constraint, an obligation. Every action on it is to by considered a duty, and not as a manner of acting which we naturally favour or might favour. (*Critique of Practical Reason*, transl. L.W. Beck, Liberal Arts Press, sometime 1956, Book 1, Chapter 3, p. 84)

> (Larry Blum's critique of Kant's Ethic (unpublished) examines these ideas in depth and develops themes discussed in his article with Marcia Homack, Judy Housman and Naomi Scheman: 'Altruism and Women's Oppression', in *Women and Philosophy,* ed. Carol Gould and Marx Wartofsky, Capricorn, 1976.)

Not only do positive social inclinations fail to measure up to the *concept* of morality, to what Kant takes to be the ordinary person's sense that morality makes an absolute and universal demand of people. Such inclinations, moreover, are at best peripheral to the attainment of human happiness on this earth and in the next. In the *Lectures on Ethics*, which together with *Education* it should be the duty of all Kant students to read, Kant writes:

> ... if none of us ever did any act of love or charity but only kept inviolate the rights of everyman, there would be no misery in the world except sickness and misfortune, and other sufferings as do not spring from the violation of rights. (*Lectures*, Harper Torchbooks (transl. L. Infield), 1963, p. 193)

Such is the bejewelled isolation of the moral life according to Kant, and, given his emotional solipsism it is no surprise to learn that he regarded masturbation as 'the most abominable conduct of which a man can be guilty' (*Lectures*, p. 170, see also *Education*, p. 117). Sexuality, that paradigm of our lower nature's anarchy, is always the *bête noire* of moralism; and masturbation, at once the supreme form of easy gratification and the standing temptation of an atomised, privatised and self-orientated society has long been its obsession. Alex Comfort's *The Anxiety Makers* and Stephen Marcus's *The*

Other Victorians, explore the activities of bodies, worthy and unworthy in this connection.

To validate morality, to make sense of the miraculous character that we have already noted even in Warnock's account, Kant had to elevate the 'pure' human will above the crass, sweaty realm of empirical causality; to split man into a celestial bureaucrat administering a bestial psychopath, to postulate an individual dignity, freedom, and rationality quite independent of wordly contingencies and to promise, in the fashion of the parish-preacher, a divine reward and penalty structure in the afterlife as dividend for the moral investment that he was calling for. We shall note below the very social and deterministic 'educational' processes which Kant proposed for the inculcation of the Free and Individual Moral Will. And we shall also be examining the utility of his anti-utilitarian 'duty-for-duty's sake' ethic for the capitalist social order. Kant's dualism powerfully reflects and firmly captures key elements in the prevailing idea of what morality is, and especially the sense, expressed even today by students to whom 'morality', like Kant himself, appears as a ghost from the credulous past, that a distinctly Moral appeal is an appeal that is from within, yet from outside, and yet again from above.

Bentham: *manager of poverty*

The power of Kant's phenomenology of morality is brought out in the backhanded deontology of those 'teleological' moralists, the British Utilitarians. I have been stressing the 'form' of moralism and the way in which Kant, with his dualism of duty and inclination, supremely articulates it.Now in one sense the utilitarians were not 'formalists'; they did not seek to ground moral duties in formal principles of 'pure reason', but in the substantial, empirical, end of 'the greatest happiness of the greatest number'. Nor did they place duty in the heavens, above earthly causality. But while their thought was devoid of Kant's idealism, the place of duty's law in the utilitarian theorists' vision of the virtuous life was scarcely less aloof and remote from direct and spontaneous passion than in the Kantian scheme. No less than his was their own thinking obsessed with abstinence, with restraint, with control,

through a law-and-ordered mind, of the dangerously seductive forces of impulse. Just as Hobbes, eschewing Divine
Right, sought to establish state-sovereignty on a footing as
firm as any devout subject might wish, so the utilitarians
sought through their psychological science (soon to be rein-
forced by Darwinism) to condemn indulgence to as dark a
hell as could be dreamt of by the most pious Victorian parson:

> To enjoy quickly - to enjoy without punishment, this is the
> universal desire of man; this is the desire which is terrible, since
> it arms all those who possess nothing against those who possess
> anything. But the law, which restrains this desire, is the most
> splendid triumph of humanity over itself. (Principles of the
> Civil Code, Chapter 9, *Bentham's Works*, ed. Bowring, Vol. 1,
> New York, 1962, p. 309)

For the utilitarians, unlike Kant, pleasure was not a
distracting lure but, along with pain, the 'sovereign master'
to whose 'governance' all mankind is wholly subject
(*Bentham*: *Principles of Morals and Legislation*, p. 1). The
monarchical irony of Bentham's expression has a real point:
in his vision inertness is man's natural state. Activity is
undertaken, not for its own sake, but for the sake of
obtaining some pleasure or avoiding some 'pain', these being
conceived of as sensations produced as more or less direct
consequences of activity: (the labour discussed in chapter
2). Naturally, then, in the interest of mimimum effort,
since effort is itself painful, mankind's first tendency
is to seek the most immediate, effortless, and readily
available pleasures. And to follow that tendency is, as
the utilitarian tracts of the nineteenth century repeat, to
follow the road to ruin, since, unlike the gratifications
produced by arduous forbearance, its fleeting pleasures bring
untold pains in tow. Hence the role of morality as one of the
road-blocks. Pleasure, for the utilitarians, was indeed a strict
ruler.

Bentham, Paley, Whateley, Bain and the others, had
contempt for nonsense on spiritual stilts; they were not
prepared to follow Kant and the plain man in seeing morality
and the conscience in terms of the mysterious contrary-to-
nature raiment in which they appear to consciousness. On the
contrary, they consistently present morality in terms of their

utilitarian psychology, and in particular in terms of social
sanctions operating through the 'association of ideas' so as to
produce pain at the thought of certain acts. Paley put it
starkly (things were expressed so much more clearly before
mass enfranchisement and literacy forced euphemism on the
ruling-class philosopher):

> As we should not be obliged to obey the laws, or the magis-
> trate, unless rewards or punishments, pleasure or pain,
> somehow or other depended on our obedience; so neither
> should we, without the same reason, be obliged to do what is
> right, to practice virtue, or to obey the commands of God... Let
> it be remembered that to be obliged is to be urged by a violent
> motive, resulting from the command of another. (*The Principles
> of Moral and Political Philosophy,* Chapter II, III, quoted in
> Selby-Bigge, *British Moralists*, Bobbs-Merrill, 1964, p. 359)

As to the precise nature of the 'sanctions of morality',
there were differences in detail among the utilitarians. Paley
seems to have stressed the feelings produced by simple
punishment for disobedience. Bentham, at least in the
Principles already referred to, stresses 'esteem', 'love',
'repute' and their opposites, together with their material
fruits, as the key to morality's development (Chapter 5,
paragraph VII; but for an extensive treatment 'of the punishments belonging to the moral sanction', see the second and
third chapters, Part II, Book 3 of 'Principles of Penal Law', in
Bentham's Works, edited by Bowring, New York, 1962, Vol.
1, p. 453). In either case morality is among the 'tutelary
motives' needing assistance in controlling the 'seductive
motives'. Bentham's dream was of a 'policed', 'superin-
tended', 'managed' capitalist society (see 'Pauper Management', *Works,* Vol. 8), and the Panopticon, designed by his
brother as a factory but offered as a model prison, was the
embodiment of his schemes of internal espionage (see Works,
1, p. 498). It was as a superintendant within each individual
that the sense of shame was to aid the legislator although, in
the case of the disorderly poor, good conduct was mainly a
function of the 'direct and constant exercise of plastic(!)
power'. In Bentham's 'Industry-Houses', then, the 'comforts
of a clear conscience, brightened by religious hopes' were to

be effected by:

> Seclusion from incentives to sin - the result of the sobriety of
> the regimen, the omnipresence of the rulers, and the mixture of
> the guardian classes of the paupers themselves with the
> susceptible classes—uninterrupted benefit of divine service;
> see below. (*Pauper Management*, Book 4)

Moral action, therefore, was action motivated by 'obligation', that is by a sense of fitness or repugnance associated
with an action through its being attended in experience with
certain socially administered pleasures and pains. There is a
blindness about it, even 'the appearance of cruelty', and the
opportunist Bentham would utilise all the authoritarian
gimmickry at society's disposal for its effective inculcation,
including the trappings of retribution:

> Render your punishments exemplary; give to the ceremonies
> which accompany them a mournful pomp; call to your assist-
> ance all the imitative arts; and let the representation of these
> important operations be among the first objects which strike
> the eyes of childhood.
>
> ... scaffold painted black... officers... dressed in crêpe... livery
> of grief... a mask... emblems of his crime... a part of the
> decorations of these legal tragedies... terrible drama... serious
> and religious music preparing the hearts of the spectators for
> the important lesson... judges preside... and its sombre dignity
> should be consecrated by the presence of the ministers of
> religion ('Indirect means of preventing crimes', 'Principles of
> Penal Law', *Works*, Vol. 1, p. 549)

The utilitarians tended to divide society into two: the
stratum of administrators of sanctions, acting consciously in
terms of the Principle of Utility (and especially its specification in Political Economy) and the stratum of administered, acting in response, on one hand to the immediate
external sticks and carrots waved about by their masters (in
the form of wages, workhouses, prisons, savings, banks,
etc.), and on the other hand to the inner prohibitions and
commands received from parents and mentors. But since
utilitarian calculation is itself far from a mere reflex, and
since, if adhered to among the masses, reflex morality is so
'utilitarian', the utilitarians were concerned that the popular-

isation of their doctrine *might* be counter-productive: in the
wrong hands, the Utilitarian Calculus could cause a lot of
mischief. Bentham urged heads of state under pressure to
avoid stimulating unmanageable reflection among the
masses:

> Every favour, everything which bears the character of benevo-
> lence, ought to be represented as the work of the father of his
> people. All rigour, all acts of severity, need to be attributed to
> no one. The hand which acts must be artfully hidden. They may
> be thrown upon some creature of imagination, some animated
> abstraction - such as justice, the daughter of necessity and the
> mother of peace whom men ought always to fear, but never to
> hate, and who always deserves their first homage. ('Principles
> of Penal Law', Chapter V, *Works*, ed. Bowring, New York,
> 1962, Vol. 1, p. 371)

A related doctrine is expressed by Henry Sidgwick, the last
of the great utilitarian theorists of the nineteenth century:

> Thus, the Utilitarian conclusion, flatly stated, would seem to
> be this; that the opinion that secrecy may render an action right
> which would not otherwise be so should itself be kept
> comparatively secret; and similarly it seems expedient that the
> doctrine that esoteric morality is expedient should itself be
> kept esoteric. Or if this concealment be difficult to maintain, it
> may be desirable that Common Sense should repudiate the
> doctrines which it is expedient to confine to an enlightened
> few. And thus a Utilitarian may reasonably desire, on
> Utilitarian principles, that some of his conclusions should be
> rejected by mankind generally; or even that the vulgar should
> keep aloof from his system as a whole, in so far as the inevitable
> indefiniteness and complexity of its calculations render it likely
> to lead to bad results in their hands. (*Methods of Ethics*,
> Macmillan, 1963, p. 490)

Act-utilitarianism for some; rule-utilitarianism for the
others. The opportunism of the utilitarian school is of course
proverbial. What I have been trying to bring out, however, is
the way this opportunism penetrates to their élitist and
authoritarian conception of the very 'form' of morality as
blind obedience to inculcated demands. Thus for example,
Hume, defending the double standard of sexual morality,
wrote of the need to instill sexual 'repugnance' in 'the ductile

minds of the fair sex in their infancy' (*Treatise of Human Nature*, III, 2, xiii).

John Stuart Mill, sometimes at least, was inclined to reject this opportunism, and this was in line with his partial attempts to develop a deeper and more adequate utilitarian theory. He recognised that the doctrine of the greatest happiness of the greatest number *could* be internalised in as blindly associative a way as any moral system, but took the view that such a mode of education, and the reflexive authoritarianism of the 'morality' it produced, was itself in conflict with the highest demands of 'utility'. Thus, at least in Chapter III of *Utilitarianism*, he argued for a moral education that would so broaden the human sympathies and understanding that 'the good of others becomes a thing naturally and necessarily to be attended to'. Among enlightened people:

> This feeling... does not present itself to their minds as a superstition of education, or a law despotically imposed by the power of society, but as an attribute which it would not be well for them to be without. (*Utilitarianism*, ed. Mary Warnock, Fontana, 1962, p. 287)

What Mill is pointing to here, and the essay *On the Subjection of Women* may be read as an amplification of the idea (rather than being consigned to the shelves as a piece of 'propaganda', as it is by sexist academics), is the connection between a deeper view of 'utility' and hence of the 'content' of morality and a radical view of the 'sanctions' proper to morality, of the 'form' of moral motivation and education. This will be taken up later.

Generally, however, the utilitarians, were far from wanting to dull the cutting edge of the puritan conscience: it was too serviceable an instrument. Many philosophers have expressed disquiet over utilitarianism, but, from Burke and Fitzjames Stephen to Devlin and even the benign Stuart Hampshire, British letters boast an honourable tradition of 'realists' who emphasise the legal and 'constitutional', that is socially enforced, character of morality as the inner barrier, sustained by fear, against the natural rapaciousness, torpor, corruptibility of the human individual. But some liberals, and expecially Mill and T.H. Green, were inclined to oppose *direct* moralistic authoritarianism, since 'enforced morality' is a 'contradition-in-terms', as Green emphasises in his *Lectures on the Principles of Political Obligation*:

> Moral duties do not admit of being so enforced. The question sometimes put, whether moral duties should be enforced by law, is really an unmeaning one; for they simply cannot be enforced. They are duties to act, it is true, and an act can be enforced; but they are duties to act from certain motives and certain dispositions, and these cannot be enforced. Nay, the enforcement of an outward act, the moral character of which depends on a certain motive and disposition, may often contribute to render that motive and disposition impossible.

Now here Green was simply following Kant's stress on the 'autonomy' of the conscientious will. As an apostle of sobriety, Green recognized that morality involved at least apparent 'self-denial' and 'the surrender of our inclination to pleasure' and that this negativity 'penetrated life' far more deeply than in the Ancient World (see *Prolegomena to Ethics*, Book III, Chapter V especially). Hence, I believe, we can see one force behind the liberal preoccupation with moral education (schooling): that activity by which children are transformed from savages (remember that Mill excludes savages and children from 'the principle of liberty' in *On Liberty*) into 'freely' self-denying adults, or rather, in the language that Green was inclined to share with F.H. Bradley, into adults who would deny their lower selves in the name of their higher selves. Thus is self-subjection transformed into a voluntary matter (and thus too we have one of the chief dimensions along with bourgeois 'liberals' differ from 'conservatives': their optimism about the Educability of Man).

B.F. Skinner; Warden of Walden

Bentham has his contemporary descendants, none more rampant than the 'behaviourists', for example H.J. Eysenck and B.F. Skinner. Eysenck:

> Our contention will be that conscience is simply a conditioned reflex and that it originates in the same way as do phobic and neurotic responses... in other words when the child is going to

carry out one of the many activities which have been prohibited and punished in the past (—the slap, the moral shaming, or whatever the punishment may be), then the conditioned automatic response would immediately occur and produce a strong deterrent, being, as it were, unpleasant in itself. (*Fact and Fiction in Psychology*, Penguin, 1965, p. 260)

Skinner, in *Beyond Freedom and Dignity* (Bantam, 1972), attacks the voluntaristic idealism of moralistic thought, assimilating it to any belief at all in mental life. Nonetheless, his book's substantial claims are all couched in thinly disguised terms of the hedonic calculus ('reward', 'aversive stimulus', etc.), and this is particularly the case in his account of moral 'training'. Skinner claims to be opposed to 'punishment' as a training 'technique' that is painful itself and also since it merely forbids without enjoining the specific behaviour desired, because it is inefficient. Thus:

> The skilful parent learns to reward a child's good behaviour rather than punish him for bad. (p. 30)

Through earning rewards, such as money, candy, television viewing-time or promotion in class, then, the child becomes conditioned to perform those operations that he has experienced as leading to reward. He becomes a well-behaved person. Ali, in Skinner's bland presentation, is groovy, especially as 'the relation between the controller and the controlled is reciprocal':

> In a very real sense the slave controls the slave driver, the child the parent, the patient the therapist, the citizen the government, the communicant the priest, the employee the employer and the student the teacher. (p. 161)

And so, too, no doubt, the caged pigeon controls the experimenter. What is concealed in Skinner's doctrine of transcendental democracy and equality, so endearing to the establishment forces that lionise him, is that the slave, child, patient, citizen, communicant, employee, student, and pigeon are likely to be in no position to make their masters do what *they* want *them* to do—to let them go, for example. They can only negotiate, within more or less narrow margins, the terms of their servitude. And this sophistical suppression of invidiousness, of the location of power in the hands control-

ling the distribution of scarce rewards, makes a mockery of
Skinner's claims to have found an 'alternative to punishment'. Skinner's is a technique of manipulation through the
exploitation of scarcity. What he does is to begin from a
position of misery, of 'zero-reinforcement' (compare God, to
whom we are supposed to owe everything), and then,
suppressing the fact that this zero-reinforcement situation is
iself set up by the 'experimenter' (teacher, prison-warden,
employer...), Skinner can pretend that all reinforcements
from there are positive, and that the worst that can happen to
the prisoner is the absence of reward (he doesn't receive any
candy, watch television or get released—it's the old authoritarian ruse of 'withdrawing privileges'). Skinner 'eliminates'
specific punishments by turning the very situation of his
subjects into a *general* punishment and offering promises of
amelioration. But in any case, if candy is established as the
reward for acceptable conduct, its pointed denial simply is a
punishment. And this Skinner himself says in a different
context, though without noticing that the point explodes his
whole thesis: 'The removal of a positive reinforcer is
aversive...' (p. 50). Skinner's cynical view of human goals,
moreover, blinds him to the fact that the candy whose
distribution his teachers are supposed to control functions to
children as a communication of approval, even love, not
simply as the source of nice taste, so that its withholding is a
form of scolding. In fact Skinner's whole system, like
Bentham's, and the management theorists' discussed earlier,
is based on the search for a technology for getting people to
do things which are intrinsically tedious. He has no place for
rewarding activities, as opposed to rewards *for* activities; or
for rewarding relations, as opposed to relations who dish out
rewards. And so, in the end, he trots out the same dualistic
structure that we found in Kant and Bentham, with 'self-
control' the ideal:

> The controlling self (the conscience or superego) is of social
> origin, but the controlled self is more likely to be the product of
> genetic susceptibilities to reinforcement (the id, or the Old
> Adam). The controlling self generally represents the interests
> of others, the controlled self the interests of the individual. (p.
> 190)

Radical Anti-Moralism from Hegel to Reich

In Britain it has been left largely to poets and novelists, such as William Blake and D.H. Lawrence, to attack the established institution of morality at its roots rather than confining themselves to criticisms of particular edicts broadcast in its name. Thus Lawrence:

> ... To be a good little boy like all the other good little boys is to be a slave... Children are all silently, steadily, relentlessly bullied into being good. They grow up good. And then they are no good...
>
> The last time I was back in the Midlands was during the great coal strike. The men of my generation were there standing derelict, pale, silent, with nothing to say, nothing to feel, and great hideous policemen from God-knows-where waiting in gangs to keep them in the lines. Alas, there was no need. The men of my generation were broken in; they'll stay on the lines and rust there. ('Enslaved by Civilization', *Assorted Articles*, London, 1930, p. 122)

On the Continent Kant's strained dualism, highlighting the tensions within moral ideology itself, came under attack almost immediately from the young Hegel. Hegel saw the repressive legalism of Kant's system, while recognising its accuracy as an articulation of the moral consciousness. He compared the paragon of moral virtue with the loyal subject of the state: the latter 'have their lord outside themselves', while the former 'carries his lord within himself'. Hegel counterposes 'the spirit of Jesus', love, to the dead heteronomy of the moral law:

> The Sermon (on the Mount) does not teach reverence for the laws; on the contrary it exhibits that which fulfils the law but annuls it as law and so is something higher than obedience to law and makes law superfluous. Since the commands of duty presuppose a cleavage and since the domination of the concept (reason) declares itself in a 'thou shalt', that which is raised above that cleavage is, by contrast an 'is', a modification of life... Against such a command Jesus sets the higher genius of reconcilibility (a modification of love) which not only does not act counter to this law but makes it wholly superfluous; it has in itself a so much richer, more living fullness that so poor a thing as law is nothing to it at all... The opposition of duty and

inclination has found its unification in the modifications of love,
i.e. in the virtues. Since law was opposed to love, not in its
content but in its form, it could be taken up into love, though in
this process it lost its shape... (Hegel: *Early Theological
Writings*, transl. Knox, Chicago, 1948, taken from *Approaches
to Ethics,* edited by W.T. Jones *et al,* McGraw-Hill, 1969, p.
331)

In *The Ego and Its Own*, the young Hegelian Max Stirner
depicted moral precepts as 'wheels in the head'. Stirner
depicted morality as the secular aftermath of religion, as the
internal echo of the Divine Father's commandments. As
such, it is all the more insidious since, through the conscientious identification of self with commander, laws 'entwine
themselves all the more inextricably with me':

To expel God from heaven, and to rob him of his 'tran-
scendence' cannot yet support a claim of victory, if thereby he
is only chased into the human breast and gifted with indelible
immanence.

Nietzsche regarded morality, with its 'intercourse between
imaginary beings' - God, the Soul, the Ego, the Will etc. - as
'mere symptomatology', the deceitful surface manifestations
of concealed anti-life forces deeply embedded in society.
Freud largely followed this way of seeing things, for all his
later conservatism:

Our civilization is, generally speaking, founded on the suppression of instincts... (but) in paying for compliance with its own
exorbitant prescriptions by increased neurosis, society cannot
claim an advantage purchased by sacrifice... Let us examine, for
example, the frequent case of a woman who does not love her
husband, because owing to the conditions of the consum-
mation of her marriage and the experience of her married life,
she has no cause to love him; but who ardently wishes to,
because this alone corresponds to the ideal of marriage in
which she has been brought up. She will then suppress in
herself all impulses which seek to bring her true impulses to
expression and contradict her ideal endeavours, and will take
particular pains to play the part of a loving, tender and
obedient wife. The result of this self-suppression will be a
neurotic illness, and this neurosis will in a short time have taken
revenge upon the unloved husband and have caused him

precisely as much trouble and dissatisfaction as would have arisen merely from an acknowledgement of the true state of affairs. ('Civilized Sexual Morality and Modern Nervousness', *Collected Papers II*, 1908, pp. 82, 98)

Later Freud developed the theory of the 'superego' to replace that of the 'ego-ideal'. Considered in its own terms as the authoritative Knower of Right and Wrong, the conscience is an illusion. Properly described, what we have here is an internalised, socially formed force, funded by the spontaneous love and hate that the little child feels for her needed but frustrating, humiliating, and threatening parents. By the time he wrote *Civilization and its Discontents*, Freud had come to focus on 'basic' aggressive rather than libidinal forces as the key to the conscience of the civilized man:

> What means does civilization employ in order to inhibit the aggressiveness which opposes it, to make it harmless, to get rid of it perhaps? What happens in the history of the development of the individual to render his desire for aggression innocuous? Something very remarkable which we should never have guessed but which is, nevertheless quite obvious. His aggressiveness is introjected, internalized... directed back towards his own ego. There it is taken over by a portion of the ego which sets itself over against the rest of the ego as super-ego, and which now, in the form of 'conscience', is ready to put into action the same harsh aggressiveness that the ego would have liked to satisfy upon other extraneous individuals.

Thus we feel 'guilt' and seek out punishment. Freudian theory shatters the illusions of autonomy of the 'conscientious' person, shifting our perspective from a rationalist, voluntarist, and idealist one to one which is psychopathological. The morally compelled person relates to his or her fellows because he or she 'must' because 'I couldn't live with myself otherwise'; he is estranged from himself, from others, and from his activities and achievements. The unquestionable character of the demands of his conscience merely echoes the unchallengeability of the social demands he has grown up to embrace as if they were his own. As John Anderson wrote:

> We should regard 'obligation' as signifying not merely a false

theory of ethics but also evil motives. Moralism, the doctrine of conscience and 'moral necessity' exemplifies the natural causality of repressive motives. There are acts which are performed under a sense of obligation but what they exhibit is not free communication but compulsion. Freud has informed us of the elaborate performances which compulsive-neurotics feel bound to go through. They are simply 'the thing to do', they are 'right' but not good, forced, not spontaneous. The spontaneous action of a motive seeking its object cannot be induced by compulsion. Compulsion can only induce uniformity. And the motives which incline a man to conform, to do a thing because he is obliged are, speaking generally, fear and the desire for self-abasement, which in sexual theory is called masochism. ('Determinism and Ethics', *Studies in Empirical Philosophy*, Sydney, 1962, essay 19, p. 225)

Common to these critics is a sense of the centrality of the 'form' of morality. Morality in this sense is a sort of violent, even thuggish suppression, rationalised as the necessary subjection of evil by good—whether the enemy is presented as 'the flesh', 'the self', 'intemperance', 'the beast (child) (savage) in us', 'the false self', 'impulses', 'the Old Adam' or even '(petty) bourgeois tendencies'. The moral 'must' is an individualistic and internalised form of social demands. To act 'morally', then, is to relate to human beings through the institutional medium of duty. Direct interactions, whether of antipathy or of sympathy, will thus be equally alien to one's second nature. Thus did Wilhelm Reich, following Freud's system but rejecting his pessimistic view of human nature, look forward to the day when the internal state would wither away as surely as the external one with which it co-operated:

When the person, in the process of gaining a different structure, realizes the indispensability of genital gratification, he loses this moralistic straight-jacket and with it the damning up of his instinctual needs. Previously, the moral pressure had intensified the impulse and made it anti-social; this in turn necessitated an intensification of moral pressure. Now when the capacity for gratification begins to equal the intensity of the impulses, *moral* regulation becomes unnecessary... The individual has no compulsive morality because he has no impulses which call for moral inhibition. (*The Sexual Revolution,* Vision Press, 1951, p. 6)

Cheap Government:
The Political Economy of Bourgeois Virtue

I have so far focused on the psychological structure, the motivational form, of bourgeois morality as presented by moralists and their critics. Indeed, like Socrates' opponents, Thrasymachus in *The Republic* and Callicles in *The Gorgias*, these critics sometimes tend to leave it at that. Even Hegel, undialectically enough, does not in this early period go into the substantial implications of a love-ethic and the trans-cendence of moral law for the *content* of life-goals, does not investigate the connection of legal form and repressive content. Stirner seems to have thought that insight and personal courage would suffice to roll the wheels of the moral 'must' out of the head and, as Marx pointed out in *The German Ideology* (see the extracts in C.J. Arthur's paper-back edition, N.Y., 1970), Stirner simply accepts the abstract dualism of moralistic thought and affirms the bourgeois ego against bourgeois morality. While Nietzsche stressed, in *The Genealogy of Morals*, that the calculable and docile moral man was the product of a process of 'civilizing' history, he tended to divide the human race into the strong supermen and the meek minions. Freud, locating the conscience's origins in the social structure of the family, increasingly came to see repression and blind guilt as the inevitable cost of 'advanced', that is, bourgeois, culture:

> ... human beings manifest an inborn tendency to negligence, irregularity and untrustworthiness in their work and have to be laboriously trained to imitate the examples of their celestial models. (*Civilization and its Discontents*, p. 55)

And even Wilhelm Reich, who did so much to bring the psychoanalytic perspective into connection with radical Marxism, tended to treat 'genital sexuality' in the narrowly biological terms of tension-reduction and not to explore the social, cultural and emotional constituents of a liberated way of life.

Marxists have often poured scorn on psychologism, the attempt to understand social problems in terms of the psychology of individuals, and as a result, as Sartre says in *The Problem of Method*, they often carry on as if workers

were born at the factory gate. But the problem is to locate
psychology, not to deny it. Thus we should indicate how,
while it constantly generates 'immorality', the capitalist
order needs 'morality' and produces it.

This is a problem; for in one sense capitalism is and is
widely seen to be an immoral system; the institutionalisation
of selfish greed. And capitalism's dawn, and the Political
Economy with which the Utilitarians trumpeted its trium-
phant passage, was and is seen as smashing the traditional
moral networks that defined feudal, paternalist, society. The
theoretical problem is addressed in Max Weber's *The Protestant Ethic and the Spirit of Capitalism* in R.H. Tawney's
Religion and the Rise of Capitalism, and E.P. Thompson's
The Making of the English Working Class works which
illuminate the issue far more than I can here. What I have
been stressing is the priority of 'form' over 'content' in the
prevailing bourgeois concept of morality, and it could be said
that Protestantism asserts this priority in its emphasis on faith
and conscience as against the stress in Catholicism on specific
manifestations of obedience in 'the good Catholic's' life.
Now it would be wrong to pretend that the repressive *form* of
morality was a protestant or bourgeois invention; the con-
quest of the flesh and other internal varieties of evil is the
bloody crusade that rages over the battlefields of western
civilization from the beginning. But 'traditional' morality's
disciplines were much more firmly bound to the performance
of specific duties and functions within a divinely ordained
'chain of being'. And it was in the name of these specific
functions and expectations ('contents') that the new bourgeois epoch was met with howls of protest and rumbles of
revolt (see E.P. Thompson, 'The Moral Economy of the
English Crowd', *Past and Present*, No. 50, 1971, and the
comment of E.G. Genovese *Past and Present,* No. 68, 1973).
Capitalism's standard is 'exchange-value', as determined
within the 'free' competitive market; that which sells, including labour, has value whatever its nature, and that which
doesn't sell is valueless. This was no mere technical abstraction (see Bishop Whately's *Lectures on Political Economy*,
1831) but legitimated a prolonged and exceedingly 'moral'
attack on the axioms of traditional morality. Thus did

capitalism turn the tables on its aged rival, with blistering irony pointing to the moral turpitude that was the other side of the coin of 'charity' and 'sympathy', hallowed virtues which, it was alleged, merely served to consecrate the vices of idleness and profligacy.

Thus it is in its harshness, its indifference, its 'appearance of cruelty', that capitalism claims its title to Morality. And it is thus in its stress on discipline, on the evils of ease and indulgent consumption, and on the stern responsibility of each for ordering his life in accordance with the harsh realities of life, that I would locate the key formal dimension of morality as it presents itself in bourgeois culture. Of course the discipline that bourgeois culture demands is structured in terms of content, latent as well as manifest. My students, for example, when asked to give examples of 'things to do with morality', mention 'not stealing' and 'telling the truth', 'respecting parents and the law'; the moral rules quoted themselves have the abstract and legal character of business propriety about them. Certainly the concern for truth-telling has little stated connection with ideas of open and communicative human relationships. In any case my impression in the classroom, as out of it, is that conscientiousness and self-denial are seen as conferring moral dignity on almost any action. As long as your actions have on them the seal of commandment, they are blessed. That is why Kant's ethics of pure form, of 'duty for duty's sake', is so liable to collapse into a capitalist and bureaucratic ethic. Certainly Kant forbade exploitation and disrespect for 'Persons', but such Beings are members of the Kingdom of Ends, whose status there is in no way compromised by their phenomenal and empirical situation in the visible world. I can respect my valet as Person while exploiting him as valet. Kant's ethics, then, merge, along with the more religious transcendentalism of puritanism, into the generalised disciplinarianism of classical capitalist morality. Capitalism and its partner since birth, the nation-state, constitute an authoritarian order, and it is by its abstract authoritarianism that the moral consciousness of this era is characterised. In military emergencies that embodiment of authority, The Nation, may command an uncashable allegiance, but in normal times it is only the 'family unit', as vehicle of authoritarian training and as focus of husbandly and wifely responsibility (through the imperatives of provision and support) that constitute a substantial sphere of concrete and sacred 'extra-economic' obligations. This sanctity has itself been subject over the years to market fluctuations, but is central to the ideology of discipline and the practice of accumulation and exploitation.

Capitalists have to compete in order to accumulate and accumulate in order to compete. Competitive drive and the capacity for disciplined abstinence are thus essential virtues of a bourgeois existence; lack of them leads the shortfaller sliding back to the wall. Ambition and self-discipline are musts, imperatives, which capitalists and career-administrators as well must obey through the subjection of feeling, spontaneity, and humanity. But, just because this competition has to be fierce, bourgeois individualism threatens mutual destruction. Thus, in partial opposition to the imperatives of ambitious drive, respect for the 'rules of the game' enshrined in law and clubbish custom ('fair play'), are necessary. This contradiction and the power of the 'success ethic' expresses itself in the fact that, even when the capitalist competitor cheats in order to win, he is commonly responding to the imperatives of his conscience. John Wesley saw another irony in the ills brought on by virtue itself; which therefore require ever stronger moral medicine:

> ... the Methodists in every place grow diligent and frugal; consequently they increase in goods. Hence they proportionately increase in pride, in anger, in the desire of the flesh, the desire of the eye and the pride of life... (quoted by E.P. Thompson in *The Making of the English Working Class*, Chapter 11)

Utilitarian Political Economy, with its doctrine of the interests of all being served by the interests of each and its obsessive onslaught on the sapping tendencies of charity and pity and of weakness and self-indulgence, provided 'scientific' underpinning to this morality. Each of us is 'responsible' for our own success or failure and each of us gets what he deserves (including the Public School place wherein to imbibe such wisdom).

Alas, the bourgeoisie and partners have not got society all to themselves. Their position rests on the lack of position of another 'sector': that which makes up the working class, that class which, we are told, whether through innate stupidity or lack of drive, has failed to invest and thus finds itself forced to labour in the factories, monuments to the saving and investment of its superiors. The top dogs, then, must control, not only their own appetites, but, even more resolutely, those of their subordinates. Now, as Bentham said, the laws of capitalist property do function 'to overcome the natural aversion to labour'; but, unless the external might of police is matched by the internal might of respect among the lower orders, property's security is slight. And unless that respect extends to a concern that the master's property or money is earned by the quality, quantity, and intensity of his own property of labour-power and labour-time the capitalist is likely to go bankrupt from the wages of supervisors. And who will supervise *them*? Forced on pain of hunger to long, hard, and tedious drudgery, without 'remnant of charm', the working class had to be turned, over time, into their own policemen, lest they played truant or rebelled against their oppressors and exploiters. The philosopher of manufacture, Andrew Ure, saw the problem in 1835:

> To devise a successful code of factory discipline, suited to the necessities of factory diligence, was the Herculean enterprise, the noble achievement of Arkwright. Even at the present day... it is found nearly impossible to convert persons past the age of puberty, whether drawn from rural or from handicraft occupations, into useful factory hands. After struggling for a while to conquer their listless or restive habits, they either renounce the employment spontaneously, or are dismissed by the overlookers on account of inattention. (*The Philosophy of Manufactures*, p. 15)

Wages, high or low, were an inadequate instrument, since the well paid workman 'irrationally' stopped working beyond what he thought of as enough, while the poorly paid workman lacked incentive to stay at the job despite the attempts of Bentham and his followers to create the threat of hell-on-earth for the unemployed. Ure had recourse to a higher paymaster:

It is, therefore, excessively in the interest of every mill-owner to organise his moral machinery on equally sound principles with his mechanical, for otherwise he will never command the steady hands, watchful eyes, and prompt co-operation, essential to excellence of product... Vague notions cannot give birth to the heroism of faith, or to self immolation for the good of others. Pure acts of virtue must be inspired by the love of a transcendent being...

Where then shall mankind find this transforming power? In the cross of Christ... it atones for disobedience; it excites to obedience; it purchases strength for obedience; it makes obedience practicable; it makes it acceptable; it makes it in a manner unavoidable, for it constrains to it; it is, finally, not only the motive to obedience but the pattern of it. (*Philosophy of Manufactures*, pp. 417, 424)

Perhaps God had better beget and have crucified a Second Son, for it would appear that piety is on the wane and that capitalists are unwilling to employ more positive motivations beyond vague appeals to teamwork; from what we have seen the recourse of participation and job-enrichment is only with reluctance turned to. At any rate, the problem has not gone away:

... The other root cause of our present difficulties with the workforce might be termed a general lowering of employees' frustration-tolerance. Many employees, particularly the younger ones, are increasingly reluctant to put up with factory conditions, despite significant improvements we've made in the physical environments in our plants. (A Ford Motor Company director, quoted in 'The Lordstown Struggle', *Solidarity Pamphlet*, 1974)

And old solutions are still with us. In October 1974, Sir Keith Joseph, intellectual spokesman of the Tory Party, called on the British Nation (in much the same spirit as the good Bishop Berkely had two hundred and fifty years before him in *The Prevention of Ruin in Great Britain*) to abandon permissiveness and the welfare bureau:

The worship of instinct, of spontaneity, the rejection of self-discipline, is not progress; it is degeneration... It was Freud who argued that repression of instincts is the price we pay for civilization... This could be a watershed in our national existence. Are we to move towards moral decline, reflected and intensified by economic decline, by the corrosive effects of inflation... Or can we remoralise our national life, of which the economy is an integral part? It is up to us, to people like you and me. (*The Guardian*, 21 October, 1974)

And a year later Archbishop Coggan of Canterbury summoned up the same forces of religion, family, authority, and self-discipline to aid the British Nation in its time of peril. Keynes said that Abstinence was the lean goddess exercising tutelage over Victorian England. His successors are calling on Her again, in the wake of the ruin of Keynesian consumerism and its soft and swinging repercussions.

Our society divides people up and presents this atomisation as the human condition; it pits them into competition with each other and calls this human nature; it demands the suppression of impulses and calls these humanity's enemy. Deficient in positive bonds, society, and even the lives of individuals, need to be held together and prevented from erupting into chaotic orgies of decadence and violence by external and internal police. If the state is God's march on earth morality is his parade on the spirit. In the absence of positive co-operative ties and positive motives to work and create, the capitalist system requires 'specialist' forces of control, armed men and harsh consciences, bullies to make us do what money alone cannot bribe us to do. Marx summed it up:

> Thus political economy—despite its worldly and wanton appearance—is true moral science, the most moral of all sciences. Self-denial, the denial of life and of human needs is its cardinal doctrine... The less you are, the more you have, the less you express your own life, the greater is your alienated life, the greater is the store of your estranged being. (*1844 Manuscripts*, Moscow, p. 119)

The Production of Morality: the Vanishing Hand of the Moral Educator

The moralist may urge us to see ourselves as 'responsible' for our 'freewill' choices, and hence to accept the blame for society's ills, but he need not be unaware of the social processes behind the individual conscience or the causes of our sense of freewill. Here are Kant's very empirical and 'phenomenal' remarks on the basic steps in producing that fine, transcendental, and noumenal member of the Kingdom of Ends, the Good Will:

> It is discipline which prevents man from being turned aside by his animal impulses from humanity, his appointed end... By discipline men are placed in subjection to the laws of mankind and brought to feel their constraint. Children, for instance are first sent to school, not so much with the object of their learning something, but rather that they may become used to sitting still and doing exactly as they are told...
>
> The love of freedom is naturally so strong in man, that, when once he has grown accustomed to feedom, he will sacrifice everything for its sake. For this very reason discipline must be brought into play very early; for when this has not been done, it is difficult to alter character in later life...
>
> We see this also among savage nations who... can never become accustomed to European manners... (*Education*, Ann Arbor, pp. 3-4)

'Break their wills betimes', as Wesley expressed it. To the moralist, the child represents all that needs to be subdued; the child is a beast, an anarchist, a bundle of drives demanding immediate gratification, a self-indulgent and irrational 'little devil'; in R.S. Peters' words, in various writings on education, especially in *Ethics and Education*, he is an 'autistic amalgam', 'a barbarian at the gate', 'an outsider'. It is on such raw and untamed material that 'moral education' sets out to do its work, and with which the conscience carries on its battle throughout life, for man is never wholly moralised; his lower self smoulders and strains and only through constant vigilance and recurrent attacks can it be kept down.

Breaking-in begins from the beginning. Few to-day would go to Wesley's limits: 'let a child from a year old be taught to fear the rod and to cry softly', but his advice to the child's moral educators, 'Begin this work before they can run alone, before they can speak plain, perhaps before they can speak at all', is widely enough heeded, as parents strive to bring their children's routines into line with their own, and employ a rich moral vocabulary in the processs (you can already hear it clearly enough in any post-natal ward). Parents judge their children as they supervise them and administer rewards for 'goodness' and punishments for 'naughtiness' though boys are expected to be a little bit naughty, as long as they are naughty in a boy's way, since their enterprise is to be harnessed later for higher things. (On the difference between the responses of parents to girls and boys, especially in Italy see *Little Girls* by Elena Gianini Belotti, (Writers and Readers Co-op, London, 1975. The conscience and the servile habit surrounding it, then, are the introjected shadow of this experience of supervision and punishment. In the monogamous nuclear family, however liberal, the child is at the mercy of her family, deprived of responsibility in the sense of determining and productive agency and denied the opportunity for full, wide, and many-sided relationships with peers and older people. Thus are imposed the isolated, anxiety-ridden, competitive character structures of the bourgeois as well as the tamed and low-aspiring character of the proletarian. Isolation, egoism, sexism, narrow sympathies and submissiveness are the natural outcome of education within the nuclear family. This is not just a function of attitudes; it can be understood only in terms of the rhythms and priorities dictated to the family unit by wider social forces, and most obviously the imperatives of male and female work. But this dictation is masked by its very banality, so that it is the family that carries the emotional burdens dumped on it by a misery-making and hostility-generating social structure. Thus for example the young adolescent's rebellion will be against his father and his individual vices, not against the system of oppression of which his frustrated father is the front-line vehicle; his son's rebellion remains 'oedipal', trapped within the narrow political limits of the family, this recurrent drama making the family a serviceable buffer. Banality masks a further, more 'normal' function: the family constitutes the narrow focus of affection and proprietary responsibility for the 'breadwinner' so that, by being brought up to confine his concerns to the family unit, the male child is being prepared to take on anything that will pay him enough to wear, before real and imaginary spectators, the badge of proud husband-and-father. By being the overloaded heart of a heartless world, the family helps keep the world heartless, and itself suffers chronic attacks.

But all children grow up and have to go to school, where stronger methods seek to cope with stronger bodies and more knowing minds, especially as many families just fail to do their job. The words of Kant are echoed by schoolmen ever since. Durkheim:

> There is a whole system of rules in the school that predetermine the child's conduct. He must come to class regularly... at a specified time and with an appropriate bearing and attitude... not disrupt... do his homework... host of obligations... It is through the practice of school discipline that we can inculcate the spirit of discipline in the child...
>
> The morality of the classroom... an intermediary between the affective morality of the family and the more rigorous morality of civil life... It is by respecting school rules that the child learns to respect rules in general. It is the first initiation into the austerity of duty. Serious life has now begun. (*Moral Education*, pp. 148-9)

Barry Sugarman:

> Impulse-control and deferred gratification is highly institutionalized in the school... further developing these patterns of control on top of the beginning which their families may have made... required to spend most of his time sitting in the required seat... not allowed to talk or freely interact with peers... Intrinsically attractive activities are supposed to be put aside in favour of others whose purpose is hard to see, but which are demanded by teachers. (*The School and Moral Development*, Croom Helm, 1973, p. 13)

R.S. Peters locates his school-ethic in the context of a Philosophy of Man:

> I conceive of the mind of the individual as a focus of social rules and functions in relation to them... wishes become wants when social standards defining ends and efficient and socially appropriate ways of attaining them become imposed on this autistic amalgam. ('The Psychology of Moral Character', in I. Scheffler ed. *Philosophy and Education*)

Education is on this view 'initiation', and Peters stresses the process whereby, as imposition deepened, individual differences are progressively ironed out:

... a child-centred approach is appropriate in dealing with the backward or difficult adolescent as it is at the infant stage... in universities... and the later stages of secondary education, the emphasis is more on the canons implicit in the forms of thought and awareness than on individual avenues of initiation... unless the idiosyncracy is so striking that the common enterprise is held up. This is one of the respects in which education differs from group therapy. (*Ethics and Education*, p. 56)

More recently Peters stresses intellectual disciplines rather than social roles as the secrets into which children are to be initiated; but the authoritarian form, the subjection of individuals to pre-given 'forms of experience', remains central, since the students are not to criticise the 'form' until they have 'mastered it'. Social roles, therefore, constitute a latent content of Peters' academicist educational philosophy. This link is clearly recognised and proclaimed in the pamphlet from the National Association of Schoolmasters, 'The Retreat from Authority' (March 1976), which condemns 'do-gooders' whose activities 'have been eroding the standards of discipline in society for a long period of time'. They call in one breath for traditional curricula and traditional modes of enforcement. (The Police Federation, ever anxious for academic excellence, welcomed the pamphlet).

The child, then, is isolated and taught to be 'good', by being taught to be 'responsible' to adult authorities, of whom, and especially of fathers and headmasters and mistresses they are commonly scared. These, then, are the sources of evaluation and retribution and hence of self-esteem and self-punishment. So is developed the intensely anxious self-surveillance and self-preoccupation of the conscientious neurotics who provided Freud with so much income and data. The 'moral education' thus imparted stands things on their head. A child hits and hurts her friend who stands howling, and the parent or teacher turns on the offending child and scolds her, ignoring meanwhile the victim's distress. The punishment actually teaches the offending child to ignore the direct impact of her actions and to focus, not on the good or harm that is the action's direct upshot, but on herself as the condemned, as the punished. Durkheim again:

> The principal form of punishment has always consisted in
> putting the guilty on the index, ostracising him, making a void
> around him, and separating him from decent people. (*Moral
> Education*, p. 175)

Established morality rests on and reinforces human isolation, turning virtues into a means to an easy conscience. In
what amounts to a wholesale rat-race of goodness, children
are encouraged to compete, on pain of isolation and contempt, for that scarce commodity, praise. Hence they acquire
a profound concern for telling tales and putting each other
down. Forbidden from co-operating on pain of 'cheating' or
of forming a disruptive solidarity ('In school, unwholesome
ferment or excitement constitutes a more serious moral
danger because the agitation is collective' (Durkheim p.
150), the children's budding moralism takes the form precisely of cheating, of putting themselves in the right against
others in order to appropriate for themselves the badges of
virtue. It presents itself too as 'collective agitation' of a
fascistic sort, in the ganging-up on moral outcasts. Thus an
uneasy selfrighteousness and an unstable identification with
the rewarding and threatening institution become the pathe-
tic payment sought from their disarmers by children deprived
of real integrity, solidarity, power, or productive agency:

> The political economy of ethics is the opulence of a good
> conscience, of virtue etc.; but how can I live virtuously if I do
> not live? (Marx, *1844 Manuscripts*)

The morality of moralism is a ghostly medium of social
exchange; it is a fantastic institution! For its particular
rewards and punishments people are brought to interact in
accordance with social demands. It rests on and reinforces a
break-down of directly motivated relations of co-operation
and reciprocity. The 'moral' man acts for the sake of his
conscience, not of his fellows, and it is only by pleasing his
conscience that the child can please himself, through pleasing
the loved and feared ones with whom he identifies. Thus are
duty and interest reconciled!

> This longing of children to be honoured and loved should be
> cultivated as much as possible... for instance, if a child tells a

lie, a look of contempt is punishment enough... (Kant, *Education,* p. 88)

Bourgeois moralism and its educationalinstitutional underpinning constitute the official apprenticeship of people for their place in our society. Without it we would be less willing to take those places. But when we do take them our moral education is not complete, for the disciplines of labour require daily imposition. We imbibe from our official institutions, then, a morality appropriate for capitalists, time-serving careerists, hacks, and rank-and-filers, a morality which detaches the focus of action from content, context and consequence (someone should form a British Society for the Social Responsibility of Moralists). It is an Eichmann morality and, judging from Stanley Milgram's experiments, it is a widely shared one. Milgram did a series of experiments, with students and others as his subjects, in which he put the subjects in the position of believing, mistakenly, that, as part of an experiment on memory, they were administering electric shocks to other 'subjects', who were in fact actors. It emerged that about sixty per cent of subjects were prepared, in response to the instructions of the experimenter, to administer shocks that produced not only screams of pain but apparent collapse. Milgram has been criticised for his willingness simply to use these people and to deceive them, and to the extent that he failed to turn this traumatically revealing experience into one of self-awareness this criticism is a just one. But Milgram did observe and question his subjects, and this is his understanding of his findings:

> The ordinary person who shocked the victim did so out of a sense of obligation—an impression of his duties as subject—and not from any particularly aggressive tendencies.
>
> It is a curious thing that a kind of 'compassion' on the part of the subject—an unwillingness to 'hurt' the experimenter's feelings—is part of these binding forces inhibiting his disobedience. The withdrawal of such deference may be as painful to the subject as to the authority he defies...
>
> The essence of obedience is that a person comes to view himself as the instrument for carrying out another person's wishes... The most far-reaching consequence is that the person feels responsible to the authority directing him, but feels no

responsibility for the content of the actions that the authority prescribes. Morality does not disappear; it acquires a radically different focus: the subordinate person feels shame or pride depending on how adequately he has performed the actions called for by authority. ('The Perils of Obedience', in *Dialogue*, April 1975)

Milgram's experiments highlight the practical upshot of the normal moral education and its authoritarian form, as a timid obedience distorts the appreciation of our actions. In terms of the formulation I have been offering, Milgram's subjects experienced a battle between the morality of 'form' and the morality of 'content', and usually it was the latter that succumbed.

Contradictions Among the People: Towards a Libertarian Socialist Ethic

Within liberalism there is a strong current of anti-authoritarianism, rooted in the idea of the possibility of spontaneous reciprocity and productivity, of the 'truly free market'. In such writers as John Dewey (see *Democracy and Education*, Macmillan, 1916) and currently Charles Silberman (*Crisis in the Classroom*, Vintage, 1971) this current beats against the stultifying authoritarianism of the schools, those 'grim and joyless places' where 'order and control are preferred over spontaneity and joy in learning' (Silberman). He urges a new morality on educators, a morality not of internalised prohibition but of 'kindness', 'gentleness', 'co-operation' and 'understanding'; and he stresses, following Dewey, that such virtues, to be communicated, have to be present as structural features of the educational experience. Silberman's description, massively researched, sets out pointedly the contrast between this and the prevailing system. His book is an essential corrective to the whitewashing sermons of Peters' British School. But Silberman's critique stays within the school walls; it fails to locate the microcosmic structure of schools in terms of their function of reproducing the dominance/submission relations that characterise our society by their certificating that society in terms of gradients of 'ability' and pigeon-holes of 'aptitude'. The competitive scramble through the tedious hoops of school and the moral education that it entails are thus resistant to change: the products of Silberman's ideal education simply would not suffer the kind of jobs our society has to offer. Freedom, as Kant saw, is no preparation for slavery, and excitement is no preparation for drudgery. Politics confined to educational radical-liberalism, then, is narrow politics.

But Silberman hints at a moral outlook and a conception of morality that differs from the dominant one that we have been surveying. This 'alternative' conception was formulated by Aristotle, according to whom moral virtue is exhibited fully only in acts toward which the agent has a direct inclination and in which he takes pleasure. Philippa Foot, to the extent that she focuses on 'virtues' rather than rules as the heart of morality, develops this way of thinking. Its point of division from the morality of 'conscientiousness' is suggested by P.H. Nowell-Smith in *Ethics*:

> ... the conscientious man will do exactly the same thing that a man who has all the natural virtues will do. He does not do them for the same reason; and he is not brave or honest or kindly, since he acts for the sake of doing his duty, not for the sake of doing the brave, honest, or kindly thing... (See the whole of Chapter 17)

While I would question this identity of content, and would urge that actions are characterised as well as caused by the spirit that infuses them (consider an obligatory smile), Nowell-Smith does draw the kind of distinction I have in mind. Bernard Harrison, in 'Fielding and the Moralists' (*Radical Philosophy* 6), shows how Fielding, in *Tom Jones*, refutes, by 'assembling reminders', the instrumental egoism of the eighteenth-century moralists, and shows Tom to act unequivocally out of compassion. The gentlemen moralists of this period, from Butler and Shaftsbury to Smith and Hume, are, however, valuable texts in developing a 'positive' or 'natural' moral philosophy, always remembering that the ethic of the 'Free Play of Mind' that Shaftsbury and his followers advocated was, like Aristotles's, for 'Gentlemen and Friends' and not for the 'mere Vulgar of Mankind' who 'often stand in need of such a rectifying Object as the Gallows before their eyes' (Shaftsbury, *Works* 1, pp. 75, 127). John

Dewey's philosophy (see *The Theory of the Moral Life* and *Democracy and Education*) and that of John Anderson (*Studies in Empirical Philosophy* and 'Art and Morality', *Australian Journal of Philosophy and Psychology,* 1941) are major carriers of the anti-moralistic tradition, praising positive virtues in contrast with the terrorised 'Virtue' exalted by the moralistic mainstream. Peter Wertheim, in an article 'Morality and Advantage' (*The Australasian Journal of Philosophy*, 1964), brings out the 'internal' rewards of virtues, and the internal miseries of vices such as envy and pride. Thus he locates morality not as a sacrificial means to peace and quiet but as a constituent of happiness.

But with the exception of Dewey and Anderson in their Marxist Phases, the 'positive moralists' tend to remain at the level of identifying 'the marks' of the good or bad man. They remain individualistic, not only in ignoring collective action (that belongs, perhaps, to 'politics'?) but in ignoring the social production (determination) of virtues and vices. These writers give the impression that the world, so far as the moral philosopher is concerned, simply consists of people with good or bad natures or with more or less success in cultivating qualities in themselves. Thus the philosophers of individual virtue abandon the task of producing good people to genetics, or to free-will, or to the upholders of educational moralism. The positive moralists, then, fail to locate goodness in the context of social ways of life; they remain trapped within the mystifying categories of individualism, within the realm of the 'moral judgement'.

Virtues and vices are attributed, not only to individual acts and individual persons, still less only to the atomic actions and persons abstracted by our philosophers and moralists ('Helping the old lady was kind', 'Smith is kind'). Collective actions, institutionalised or informally organised whole ways of life, can be generous or cruel just as much as individual acts can be. Recognising this and with it the fact that human action typically occurs, if not in direct association at least in a social context, we can feel the pull toward using 'morality' with a wider scope of reference. I have argued for thinking of 'the political' as penetrating the microcosms of social life and would argue for a conception of 'morality' that sees it penetrating the macrocosms. Whether or not some further specification might be called for, 'morality', I would urge, can be fruitfully used to refer to a very broad and inclusive field: to good and evil in respect of human activity. In this sense, when I have been attacking the evils of 'morality' in the established sense, I have been moralising. Is it too banal to note the directly social meaning of the Greek and Latin roots of 'ethics' (ethos) and 'morality' (mores)? Dewey tried to express this wider notion thus: 'ethics'

> ... has to study the inner process as determined by the outer conditions or as changing those conditions, and the outward behaviour or institution as determined by the inner purpose, or as affecting the inner life. (*Theory of the Moral Life*, Introduction)

Moralism begins with a myth about human nature and the need to conquer it (paradigmatically in its sexual expression) for higher ends, concealing that this 'nature' and the 'ends' for which it has to be quelled are equally socially and historically patterned. I have emphasised the way in which Morality with a big 'M' functions to batter people down into acquiescing in the poverty that passes for their lot in our society, and how it domesticates people into an instrumental sociability in the quest for a quiet conscience; how its Incentive-to-Goodness Plan operates. But, starting in another way we can, perhaps, make sense of the realities which moralism exploits while it distorts them. I offered a provisionally general 'definition' of morality as the term covering issues of good and evil in respect of human activity. The utter width of this 'definition' has at least this in its favour: unlike the narrow conception of moralism, it does not preempt the answer to questions as to the roots of good and evil in life. Moralism is in fact a substantive answer to the question: it blames everything on 'lack of moral standards' and so on. Now it should be clear that I do not accept this. But there is, I think, a 'truth' in moralism that it articulates in a twisted way. I have stressed the repressive form of the moralists' morality. But must we think in terms of repression and of the duty/inclination dichotomy to see morality as involving an essentially 'negative form'? Why is it natural to think of kindness as a moral virtue and not affection? Aristotle said that each moral virtue involved the mastery of a particular passion in circumstances where giving into that passion would be bad. Morality seems to have its home in a context of 'temptation'. And kindness, for example, involves a complex relation between the appreciation of some people's need and the contending disposition not to give up some personal good for the sake of meeting that need. Now it is easy to present this as a situation of 'duty versus inclination', but there is no reason at all why we should not think of the kind person as moved by direct concern and sympathy, as therefore positively 'inclined' to help. But, by contrast with a human virtue such as love or sympathy which has its target in a 'simple' way, a person is thought to be kind, and is thus 'morally' characterised, in virtue of a relationship among his dispositions. After all, if she did not value that for herself which she is disposed to give, she would not be 'kind' to give it. The way 'love' or 'sympathy' belongs to 'the language of morals', then, would be in terms of its place in the organisation of a person (or collectivity's) motives or dispositions (A.F. Shand's *Foundations of Character*, 1914, W. Reich's *Character Analysis*, and F. Perls, R. Hefferline and P. Goodman's *Gestalt Therapy,* 1951, remain mines of insight about the 'political' relationships among the passions). I have concentrated on virtues of individuals to make this point, but it is one that can be generalised. If we begin not with the moralist's myth about 'human nature' and its base impulses but with the desirability of co-operation in conditions of at least relative scarcity, we could think of morality in terms of this co-operation. For 'scarcity' means that some things and activities are restrained, given up, or underdeveloped, and that some desires cannot be satisfied; scarcity entails 'limits', 'discipline', 'organisation', restraint', not only between people, but within them. 'Morality', then, simply is 'politics' under the aspect of good and evil. And it is possible, I suggest, to understand this, and the 'contradictions among the people' inevitably connected with it, in ways that socialists and lovers of freedom can accept.

To talk of morality in this 'non-moralistic' way, it seems to me, would be to talk in terms, not of a higher power, an authoritative voice, controlling our inclinations, but rather of the relation among our activities (dispositions, impulses, inclinations, feelings, passions, values) as they are formed and expressed by our ways of life. It is in these non-moralistic terms that I have been trying to understand the moralistic conscience itself. Thus, for example, 'restraint' would be understood not in terms of the action of some 'higher' force but (remembering that restraint is mutual, that it is often bad, and that it can occur for the most 'selfish' reasons, like not wanting to be sick in the morning) in terms of tendencies giving in to stronger ones with which they are on some occasion incompatible. And 'socialist restraint' would be, very crudely, the preponderance of communal, productive, loving, and communicative activities and motives over invidiously divisive (including moralistic) activities and motives. And I am explicitly thinking of such relationships as occurring both within and among people, groups (classes, sexes, races), institutions and societies. Ways of living can be morally characterised; they can, for example, be cooperative or divisive and exploitative, free or compelled and authoritarian, open-hearted or envy-ridden, communicative or repressive. And, from a radical-materialist standpoint, we can attempt to (causally) understand such ways of life and also to be able to sort out the role of ideological masks, such as moralism, in constituting and maintaining them. Writing of the 'traditional' classroom, Dewey exemplifies this radical materialism:

> ... I think it is fair to say that one reason the personal commands of the teacher so often played an undue role and a reason why the order that existed was so much a matter of sheer obedience to the will of an adult was because the situation almost forced it on the teacher. The school was not a group or community held together by participation in common activities. Consequently, the normal, proper conditons of control were lacking. Their absence was made up for, and to a considerable extent had to be made up for, by the direct intervention of the teacher, who as the saying went, 'kept order'. He kept it because order was in the teacher's keeping, instead of residing in the shared work being done. (*Experience and Education*, 1938, Collier 1963, p. 55)

'Socialist restraint'? I have been attacking the authoritarian form of bourgeois moralism, but there is undoubtedly a 'socialist' moralism that 'represses each in the interests of all' (in fact in the interests of such developments as are suited, for example, to the dominant cliques and bureaucracies of such states as the U.S.S.R.). So there needs to be some clarification and some recognition of the danger of insidiously reproducing the rejected in an acceptable guise. What I am concerned with, then, is a socialist form corresponding to a socialist content; and what motivates this concern is the recognition that in those societies where 'socialist morality' is to a greater or lesser degree imposed through an education in repression, its outcome in terms of content is an undemocratic, servile, and egoistic mockery of socialism. No doubt compulsion is ineradicable from political life; but it reflects ill on a society's dominant goals that compulsion is the principal means of securing them.

I have been stressing the poverty, misery, and inequality bound up with the capitalist mode of production and the consequent role of the state and its laws, of schools, of families, and of the very organisation of work itself in maintaining or reproducing this system. Clearly, then, to the extent that productive life, and reproductive life too, are themselves pleasurable and fulfilling rather than joyless and frustrating, the need for compulsion and its internal vehicle the dutiful conscience 'withers away'. Further, to the extent that the mode of production and reproduction itself depends on conscious cooperation and mutual aid rather than hierarchical regulation and invidious competition, 'sociability', in the emotional form of sympathy and the spirit of comradeship, is fostered as a virtue directly aiming at 'the common good' in a way that the policed sociability of repressive morality, by which 'the good' is to be sought only as a duty, positively hinders. A socialist way of life, then, abstractly presented to be sure, is one which, as cooperation supplants compulsion, involves an inversion of 'morality', from an authoritarian to a free mode.

It is not a question only of 'reducing' repression; nor can we expect, with Reich, that in the good society there will be something like a full harmony of impulses. What I want to

stress is that there are alternatives to coercion and specifically to moralism, even in connection with forces, tendencies, dispositions that are bad (greed, envy, possessiveness,
domination) or whose being acted on in a particular situation would be bad. Since I am arguing that one such
tendency is moralism itself it would be ironic if the position
advocated were to amount to a call for its repression! Rather,
taking up with Freud the liberal notion of the 'open society'
and applying the critique of censorship (repression) that it
entails to the dynamics of personality, we should recognise
the ineradicability of painful 'contradictions' both among and
within 'the people' and consider the existence of alternatives
to the weapons of moralism for 'handling these contradictions correctly' (the expression is Mao Tse-tung's and 'On the
Correct Handling of Contradictions among the People' is
valuable, if ambiguous, reading in this context). Moralism
aspires, hopelessly, to destroy its enemy through punishment, censorship, denial, contempt. Like its public embodiment, the judge-in-court, it avoids the struggle to com-
municate, understand, question, and criticise, let alone to
trust and respect. It condemns 'out of hand', while at the
same time abandoning 'the repressed', like the prisoners
created by the judiciary, to smoulder in bitter isolation
dreaming of revenge, their threat and cost to society mounting even as they are held secure to 'pay the price' of their
crime. It is from schools of psychotherapy most removed
from an authoritarian and coercive psychiatric perspective
that most is to be learned here. Perls, Hefferline, and
Goodman write in *Gestalt Therapy*:

> In... development... there were conflicting tensions, but the
> conflicts worked themselves out - with disruptions of habits,
> destruction, assimilation, and a new configuration. Now
> suppose the situation has been a blocked one: e.g. suppose the
> genital primacy was not strongly established because of oral
> unfinished situations, genital fears, so-called 'regressions', and
> so forth. And suppose all the contestants are brought out into
> the open, into open contact and open conflict, with regard to
> object-choices, social behaviour, moral guilt on one hand and
> affirmation of pleasure on the other. Must not this conflict and
> its attendant suffering and hardship be the means of coming to

a self-creative solution? ...If the solution is pre-conceived and
forwarded by the therapist... much suffering and danger may
be avoided; but the solution will be so much more alien and
therefore less energetic. That is, it is unwise to allay the conflict
or suppress or interpret away any strong contestants, for the
result must then be to prevent a thorough destruction and
assimilation, and therefore to condemn the patient to a weak
and never perfectly self-regulating system. (Chapter IX 'Conflict and Self-conquest', pp. 357-8)

Moralism feasts on mistrust, fear, and hatred, of self and
others; and it is a commonplace of therapy, especially in the
psychoanalytic schools, that such layerings are the prime
obstacle to growth and health, and that the therapeutic
process is therefore in large measure one in which the erosion
of these inward and outward-directed blocks, mutually
engendering, enables people to establish 'contact with their
feelings' and with others and to gain the courage to 'work
through' or at least to come to terms with their vices and
genuinely to 'control' them. The specialised practice of
'therapy' (I am not talking about those spiritual marines, the
orthodox psychiatrists and aversion therapists) is therefore in
many respects a model of the generalisable social practice of
healing, of supportive mutual criticism, (and moralism
makes people terrified of criticising or being criticised) that
constitutes the practical alternative to moralism. Friends,
more or less timidly, already practice therapy in this sense,
and while often moralistic towards males, the women's
movement, in consciousness-raising groups and peer-
counselling, is already evolving and testing out non-
moralistic, non-repressive ways of 'handling contradictions',
of opening up communication among and within. Thus is the
struggle for liberation itself liberating, and this remains its
tendency despite the obvious fact that it entails a protracted
and at times bloody war with the forces of oppression, forces
that cannot be eroded by dialogue but that have to be
confronted, to an extent, in their own terms of coercive force.
Here one can only say that, to the extent that the militancy
and discipline necessary for this struggle become crystallised
into an 'ethic' of authoritarian militarism and moralistic
hatred and resentment, the revolutionary process will itself

throw up forces inimical to liberation.

Marx wrote in the Third *Thesis on Feuerbach* attacking the idea of a dichotomy between those 'superiors' who change social circumstances and those who are changed by them, and affirmed 'the coincidence of the changing of circumstances and of human activity' in 'revolutionary practice'. In the *1844 Manuscripts*, moreover, he sketches the process by which the need of workers to come together and organise against their alienation generates the expansion of sympathies to the point that the overthrow of oppression becomes neither a means to selfish gain nor yet a moral 'imperative' working through guilt and self-denial, but a demand of the workers' 'being':

> When communist workmen associate with one another, theory, propaganda, etc., is their first end. But at the same time, as a result of this association, they acquire a new need - the need for society - and what appears as a means becomes an end... Company, association, and conversation, which again has society as its end, are enough for them; the brotherhood of man is no mere phrase with them but a fact of life, and the nobility of man shines upon us from their work-hardened bodies. (Moscow edition, pp. 124-5)

By contrast Marx argued that the mode of life of the bourgeois and of the French peasants precluded this co-operativeness and humanistic solidary spirit. And it is to this ethic of spontaneous discipline, 'spontaneous' in a sense that clashes not with leadership so much as with authoritarian commandism, that Rosa Luxemburg refers in her 1904 polemic against Lenin:

> He (Lenin) glorifies the educative influence of the factory, which, he says, accustoms the proletariat to 'discipline and organization'... The discipline Lenin has in mind is being implanted in the working-class not only by the factory but... by the entire mechanism of the centralized bourgeois state.
>
> We misuse words and we practise self-deception when we apply the same term—discipline—to such dissimilar notions as: 1, the absence of thought and will in a body with a thousand automatically moving hands and legs, and 2, the spontaneous co-ordination of the conscious political acts of a body of men. What is there in common between the regulated docility of an oppressed class and the self-discipline and organization of a

class struggling for its emancipation? (*Leninism or Marxism?*, Ann Arbor, 1961, p. 90)

This capitalist political discipline remains a virulent current in the revolutionary movement to-day as parties, sects and individuals struggle to temper themselves into steel hammers to 'smash' the obstacles to socialist revolution, succeeding often enough only in burning themselves up and sending would-be converts running to find the shelter of bourgeois peace-and-quiet. Picking up from Reich's criticism of the communist movement of the 1930s, Michel Schneider attempts to analyse the 'political psychology' prevalent among many Marxist sects of Europe today:

> Since these comrades have sacrificed yesterday's (petty) bourgeois joys to to-day's 'correct proletarian line', they harbour a secret hatred for the political work which imposes this sacrifice on them... Such a political movement, whose subjective motivating force is derived chiefly from petty-bourgeois aggressions and guilt-feelings and which fails to release libidinal counter-tendencies, cannot create a revolutionary cultural milieu in which student and worker comrades would treat each other as equals and not as political rivals. It is therefore, a movement which invests all its energy in a purely negative practice without developing to any significant extent the positive side through the socialization and 'proletarianization' of its internal relations. Not surprisingly it has great difficulty in winning the sympathy of the proletarian masses.
>
> All this is particularly harmful for a socialist movement, since the punitive and penitential character that political work assumes for any student comrades also manifests itself in the content of political action and propaganda. (*On Left-Wing Dogmatism, A Senile Disorder*, transl. from the German, available from Rising Free, London, or Liberation, U.S.A.)

Within the socialist movement, then, there are powerful tendencies to reproduce the repressive structures of capitalism in a dualism of organisers and organised that penetrates from the level of the party to that of the individual psyche. But if 'the left' in the west is to be not a posterior phenomenon of capitalism but prefiguration of socialism, it will have to get beyond the point of oscillating between presenting socialism in terms of a good consumer deal (economism) and in terms of a moral imperative (moralism). And that is why Schneider is right, it seems to me, in stressing the need for 'positive' politics, politics which affirm and embody in the here-and-now the values which the socialist movement is a movement towards. This prefiguration is in any case an objective fact and those hard-headed political engineers who freeze at the mention of 'spontaneity' do not realise, in their faith that the centralist managers of the revolutionary process will 'in due course' see fit to surrender their control as if they stood outside the historical movement, that they are the true utopians. Here Luxemburg was absolutely right: Lenin's 'revolutionary discipline' lives on in the Soviet factories, schools, and families to this day. That Marx's early optimism has not been fulfilled, that the working class in the west has not been the unequivocal embodiment of 'the brotherhood of man' and has not, for reasons that are themselves broadly explicable within Marx's own framework, already emerged as an irrepressibly revolutionary force in society, is no reason to turn in despair to the politics of putchism and moralism, politics which has the same fetishistic logic as prison-mania: it achieves nothing, but 'something must be seen to be being done'.

Capitalist moralism, its constant grind and its recurrent frenzy, is itself a symptom of the insecurity of a system based on repression—on the need to turn human potential into labour-power, on the need to turn the love of joy into the terror of failure. The weight of the lid, then, is a measure of the pressure below it, in the form especially of unmanageable instincts, unmanageable labourers, and unmanageable children to boot. Thus it is absurd, 'undialectical', to present official morality as exercising the control that it pretends to on speech-nights. The more recent forms of what Marcuse calls 'repressive tolerance' and 'repressive desublimation' (see *One Dimensional Man*) attempt to take the sting out of people's frustrated desires and needs, not by directly attacking them, but by selling packaged partial satisfactions, Playmates-of-the-Month. They do so, however, at the cost of generating desires that cannot be contained in bourgeois packages. So moralism itself generates the rebellion whose quelling is its official mission. Thus are the contradictions that we found in 'scientific management' and 'job-enrichment' general problems of class rule. There is never a time when the world is not going to the dogs. Even in the best-regulated nations the dominant order is threatened, and official morality is a mark of this threat. The oppressed associate, organise, and resist. Certainly, as is so clear within the trade union movement, these organisations can incorporate precisely what the oppressed classes are up against. But people organise at a more spontaneous level; on the job and in neighbourhoods, through the experience of common suffering and common resistance. No wonder the patrons of our society are so anxious to rescue the decent individual workman from mob-rule (when they aren't concerned to rescue the decent majority from the few politically motivated extremists!). Nor are even the best-regulated families or schools the seamless moral webs they advertise themselves to be; their morality is to be found in the texture and contradictions of everyday practice, not in their precepts. To the extent, for example, that there are affectionate and communicative relationships within a family and that these extend beyond its walls, positive 'moral education' goes on through the informal medium of sympathy and example. Unofficial moral education goes on in all sorts of ways as, for instance, when a child is aware that 'something is wrong' between her officially happy parents and seeks to understand it and intervene; as for instance, when the child forms friendships against the drift of parental reserve or hostility. Brick walls, the 'moral architecture' of our culture, stand against these free explorations, sexual and otherwise. And, especially at schools, the fact that children develop active relations with each other, independent and often critical of adult hegemony with its demand for corporate identification and individual competition, makes for a more or less autonomous, if submerged, 'morality'. It is a morality that the herders of Big-M Morality, with their onslaught on 'bad company', struggle to contain and crush, imposing the atomisation of corporate 'roles' in the so-called 'socialization process'. This 'problem' is particularly chronic in working-class schools where more and more children are refusing to

play the game in which they are already cast as the losers:
better to lose without the deceit that you 'did your best'. And
it is no longer such an easy task to raise pillars of society
among the children of the 'upper' classes, as can be seen by
the relatively unblinkered way in which students survey the
alternatives to the lonely obedience-career path that their
parents and teachers have given all to lay down. While the
established left continues to strive to wring socialism predominantly out of the wage-struggles of workers, it is, in my
view, from critical immersion in the scattered, often fragile,
struggles against the despotism of capitalist and state
authorities and for collective self-management, democratic
production and fulfilment that the revolutionary movement
can rise to strength and coherence. It is in that context that
the struggle against bourgeois moralism needs to be fought,
for it is in that context that the erosion of bourgeois ties can
lead to their being supplanted, not by passive bourgeois
cynicism but by active socialist passion.

INDEX

A

Althusser, L. 35
Amos, M. 91
Anderson, J. 149-50, 166
Arendt, H. 26, 63, 86
Argyris, C. 68
Aristolle, 26
Augustine, 109
Austin J. 93-5
Ayer, A. J. 124

B

Bakunin, H. 27-8
Bao-Ruo-wang, 47
Beeton, I. 65
Bell, D. 63
Belotti, E. G. 159
Benn, S. I. 15,46
Benn, T. 65
Bentham, 54, 95, 101, 110, 113,
    138-142, 146, 155
Berkely, G. 156
Berlin, I. 56
Blake, W. 147
Blum, L. 137
Bosanquet, B. 12
Bradley, F. H. 144
Braverman, H. 63
Bullock, A. 60, 81-85
Burke, E. 34, 92

C

Callaghan, J. 22
Carey, A. 67
Carr, R. 80
Castle, B. 80
Child, J. 76
Chinoy, E. 69
Clayre, A. 55, 70
Clegg, H. 57, 71
Coggan, J. 157
Colby, W. 97
Cole, G. D. H. 27
Comfort, A. 137

D

Dahl, R. 21
Dewey, J. 54-5, 68, 164, 166, 167,
    169
Diamond, S. 105

Doppelt, G. 48
Durkheim, E. 91, 133-135, 160,
    161-2

E

Easton, D. 21-2
Engels, F. 12, 28, 33, 70
Epicurus, 25
Eysenck, H. J. 144-5

F

Figgis, J. N. 20
Fitzgerald, M. 118
Foot, P. R. 123
Freud, S. 148-9, 151
Friedman, M. 17, 27
Fromm, E. 68
Fuller, L. 97

G

Genovese, E. G. 152
Gibbs, B. 56
Gluckman, M. 115
Goldmann, L. 130
Goldring, J. 106-7
Goodman, P. 168, 171-2
Gorz, A. 64
Gramsci, A. 35
Green, T. H. 144

H

Hampshire, S. 128
Haraszti, M. 87
Hare, R. M. 125
Harrison, B. 165
Hart, H. L. A. ql.ff. 111, 118, 128
Hay, D. 96, 98-9
Hefferline, R. 168, 171-2
Hegel, G. W. F. 147-8
Hendel, C. 13-14
Henriques, U. R. Q. 118
Herzberg, F. 68, 69, 76
Homak, M. 137
Honderich, T. 110
Housman, J. 137
Hume, D. 95

I

Illich, I. 89

J

Jenkins, C. 74
Joseph, K. 156

K

Kamenka, E. 132
Kant, I. 8, 110, 136-8, 153, 158, 162-3
Kropotkin, P. 118, 112-13

L

Lawrence, D. H. 147
Lenin, V. I. 37, 70, 132, 173
Likert, J. 68
Lucas, J. R. 15
Lucas Shop Stewards Committee 79
Luxemburg, R. 173, 175

M

McGahey, M. 22
McGregor, D. 66
Malinowski, B. 115
Mandel, E. 71
Mao Tse-tung, 171
Marcus, S. 137-8
Marcuse, H. 175
Marx, K. 18, 28-34, 38, 62, 129-33, 157
Maslow, A. 68
Mayo, E. 66
Mihajlov, M. 118
Milgram, S. 163
Miliband, R. 35
Mill, J. S. 64, 143
Mitford, J. 118, 120
Morris, H. 111-12, 118
Morris, W. 45

N

Nadel, S. F. 106
Nietzsche, F. 135, 148, 151
Nixon, R. 98
Norman, R. J. 126
Nowell-Smith, P. H. 165
Nozick, R. A. 48-53

P

Paley, W. 95, 97, 139-40
Perls, F. 168, 171-2
Peters, R. S. 15, 23, 46, 134, 158, 160
Plato, 8, 25-6
Poulantzas, N. 35

Q

Quinton, A. M. 19

R

Ramelson, B. 60
Rawls, J. 17, 46-8
Reich, W. 41, 150, 151, 168, 170
Revans, R. W. 55, 65, 74, 77
Roberts, B. 59
Rosenstein, E. 72
Rothman, D. 116-17
Runciman, W. G. 27
Russell, B. 132
Ryle, G. 54

S

Saint-Simon, H. 27
Salmond, J. W. 92
Sartre, J. P. 151-2
Scheman, N. 136
Schneider, M. 174
Schram, S. 72
Shaftsbury (3rd) 165
Shand, A. F. 168
Sidgwick, H. 142
Silberman, S. 164
Skinner, B. F. 109, 144-6
Smith, A. 17, 62
Sorel, G. 28
Stevenson, C. 124
Stirner, M. 148, 151

T

Tawney, R. H. 152
Taylor, F. W. 61, 71-3
Thompson, E. C. 98, 152
Tocqueville, A. 116
Trotsky, L. 49, 70, 132

U

Ure, A. 62, 155-6

W

Warnock, G. J. 123, 125
Weber, M. 20, 152
Wertheim, P. 166
Wesley, J. 154, 158
Whately, R. 151, 152
Wilson, H. 22, 81
Wiseman, H. V. 21
Wittgenstein, L. 10

22/11X